Tech Requ

[handwritten: Purpose → guide]

In this much-needed book, experts Emily L. Davis and Brad Currie draw on their extensive experience in coaching and instructional technology and provide concrete, research-based strategies to help coaches in their day-to-day role. Whether you're beginning a coaching initiative or looking for practical insights on coaching in a variety of settings, including in groups and one-to-one, you'll find the resources you need to overcome challenges and grow your coaching skills.

Topics include:

- The basics of tech coaching
- How to clarify on the expectations and objectives of your role
- Tips for recruiting teachers to work with you
- Guiding educators in planning and implementing meaningful technology integration
- How to plan and facilitate effective team coaching
- Strategies to gather and share data to communicate the impact of your coaching work
- How to stay ahead of the curve and keep learning for the future

Every chapter includes practical tools, templates, and illustrative vignettes from the field to help you ensure the success of your technology coaching initiative.

Join the conversation! Discuss the book and your coaching questions on Twitter with the hashtag #TechRequestEDU.

Emily L. Davis, Ph.D. (@mentorEmily), is an expert on the development of high quality induction and coaching programs for both new and experienced teachers. After research and leadership roles at Stanford, New Teacher Center, and the Santa Cruz/Silicon Valley New Teacher Project, she is now the co-founder of the Teacher Development Network which helps districts and states leverage the power of preservice and inservice mentoring to improve recruitment, teaching, and learning.

Brad Currie (@TheBradCurrie) has been an educator for more than 18 years as a coach, teacher, and administrator. He currently serves as a Director of Planning, Research, and Evaluation for the Chester School District in Chester, New Jersey. He is the co-founder and co-moderator of a weekly Twitter discussion for educators called #satchat.

Also Available from Routledge Eye On Education

(www.routledge.com/k-12)

Connecting Your Students with the World: Tools and Projects to Make Global Collaboration Come Alive, K-8
Billy Krakower, Paula Naugle, Jerry Blumengarten

Getting Started with STEAM: Practical Strategies for the K-8 Classroom
Billy Krakower and Meredith Martin

10 Perspectives on Innovation in Education
Edited by Jimmy Casas, Jeffrey Zoul, Todd Whitaker

Intentional Innovation: How to Guide Risk-Taking, Build Creative Capacity, and Lead Change
A.J. Juliani

Inquiry and Innovation in the Classroom: Using 20% Time, Genius Hour, and PBL to Drive Student Success
A.J. Juliani

Active Literacy Across the Curriculum: Connecting Print Literacy with Digital, Media, and Global Competence, K-12
Heidi Hayes Jacobs

The Mathematics Coaching Handbook: Working with K-8 Teachers to Improve Instruction, 2nd Edition
Pia M. Hansen

The STEM Coaching Handbook: Working with Teachers to Improve Instruction
Terry Talley

The Literacy Coaching Handbook: Working with Teachers to Increase Student Achievement
Diana Sisson and Betsy Sisson

Tech Request

A Guide for Coaching Educators in the Digital World

Emily L. Davis
Brad Currie

Routledge
Taylor & Francis Group

NEW YORK AND LONDON

First published 2019
by Routledge
52 Vanderbilt Avenue, New York, NY 10017

and by Routledge
2 Park Square, Milton Park, Abingdon, Oxon, OX14 4RN

Routledge is an imprint of the Taylor & Francis Group, an informa business

© 2019 Taylor & Francis

Library of Congress Cataloging-in-Publication Data
Names: Davis, Emily L., author. | Currie, Brad, author.
Title: Tech request : a guide to coaching educators in the digital age /
    Emily L. Davis, Ph.D., Brad Currie.
Description: New York : Routledge, 2019. | Includes bibliographical
    references.
Identifiers: LCCN 2018054202 (print) | LCCN 2019002619 (ebook) |
    ISBN 9780429486036 (ebook) | ISBN 9781138598898 (hbk) | ISBN
    9781138598904 (pbk) | ISBN 9780429486036 (ebk)
Subjects: LCSH: Education—Effect of technological innovations on. |
    Educational innovations. | Mentoring in education.
Classification: LCC LB1028.3 (ebook) | LCC LB1028.3 .D288 2019
    (print) | DDC 371.33—dc23
LC record available at https://lccn.loc.gov/2018054202

ISBN: 978-1-138-59889-8 (hbk)
ISBN: 978-1-138-59890-4 (pbk)
ISBN: 978-0-429-48603-6 (ebk)

Typeset in Palatino
by Swales & Willis Ltd, Exeter, Devon, UK

Dedication

Brad would like to dedicate this book to the remarkable instructional coaches that he works with in the Chester School District. Their passion for technology, literacy, and mathematics is tremendous and directly tied to the amazing teaching and learning that takes place on a daily basis. Keep fighting the good fight! Thank you also to my wonderful wife Leigh who constantly supports my efforts as an author and speaker. Finally, to my son Cooper and daughter Sydney who I love to the moon and back. May your schools always have awesome instructional coaches who care deeply about engaging learning environments.

Emily would like to express her gratitude to the mentors, instructional coaches, and leaders connected with the Santa Cruz/Silicon Valley New Teacher Project. Your tireless work on behalf of teachers and students is inspiring. I am so much smarter for having worked with you! Thank you also to my husband and daughters for your patience as I have spent nights and weekends away from you writing this book. I couldn't have done it without your love and support.

Contents

Figures and Tables

Meet the Authors

Emily L. Davis, Ph.D. is the co-founder of the Teacher Development Network. She began her career as a middle and high school humanities teacher in a variety of states before earning her Ph.D. in Curriculum and Instruction from the University of Virginia. She has developed, run, and researched a number of induction programs across the country including at Stanford University. Most recently, Emily served as the program director for the Santa Cruz/ Silicon Valley New Teacher Project and as a Senior Director at New Teacher Center. She is a sought-after consultant, speaker, and professional developer on topics including mentoring, coaching, facilitation, and professional learning. She is the author of numerous articles and blogs on teacher mentoring, induction, and coaching topics. Her previous book, *Making Mentoring Work*, is a practical guide for school leaders looking to begin or enhance their mentoring programs for new teachers. Dr. Davis has also been nationally recognized by both Phi Delta Kappa and ASCD as an Emerging Leader in the field of education. You can connect with Emily on Twitter @mentorEmily or by visiting her company's website at www.teacherdevelopmentnetwork.com.

Brad Currie has been an educator for more than 18 years as a coach, teacher, and administrator. He currently serves as the Director of Planning, Research, and Evaluation for the Chester School District in Chester, New Jersey. Brad is the 2017 NASSP National Assistant Principal of the Year and part of the ASCD Emerging Leaders Class of 2014. He is the co-founder and co-moderator of a weekly Twitter discussion for educators called #satchat. Brad has authored four books including *140 Twitter Tips for Educators* and *Hacking Google for Education*. He presents nationally on leadership, teaching, and learning in the digital era. Brad is a Google Certified Trainer and supports districts in implementing Google Apps for Education. Connect with Brad by following him on Twitter @TheBradCurrie or visiting his company website at www.evolvingeducators.com.

Foreword

Technology and connected learning continue to be a topic filled with great debate, which seems so strange because they have been a part of our educational community for over 20 years. In fact, I remember when every classroom in our school was equipped with four computers. It was in the mid-90s in my third year of teaching. Many of us were so excited to receive the computers because we knew that technology was the wave of the future. I mean, I was a kid who grew up with a Commodore VIC-20, learned how to code my own design that took hours to create, so I was all excited to have computers in the classroom. The only issue was that we lacked the knowledge needed to incorporate the large desktops into our everyday instructional practices and none of us were ever provided with professional development on how to do so. This continues to be an issue for educators, and it's having a negative impact on how they approach digital learning.

As an author and consultant, I have had the opportunity to work with John Hattie for the last five years. Hattie provides us with the largest database of research in education. He has synthesized over 1,400 meta-analyses which include over 256 influences and effect sizes related to student achievement. Some of those influences are classroom practices like feedback, reciprocal teaching, and classroom discussion. One of the influences Hattie has paid attention to is one-to-one tablets. Just like the explosion of schools that wanted to bring computers into classrooms, there was a similar explosion of school leaders who wanted to bring in one-to-one initiatives and put a tablet in the hands of every student. This seemed like a great idea, but when we began to scratch the surface, we found that one-to-one initiatives did not provide the bang for the buck school leaders were hoping for. In fact, Hattie's research shows that one-to-one initiatives have an effect size of 0.16, which is well below the hinge point of 0.40 that equates to a year's worth of growth for a year's input.

It's odd isn't it? Why is it that more than 20 years after computers were first brought into classrooms, one-to-one initiatives aren't very successful? After all, nearly every educator who teaches has a personal smartphone, and many are connected to various forms of social media. Yet when those same educators enter into the classroom, only a fraction of them interweave technology into their classroom strategies successfully. Once again, the issue is the professional development that doesn't always come with these great initiatives.

Of course, all of this does not mean we simply ban digital devices from the classroom. Just because Hattie's research shows that one-to-one devices have a low effect size doesn't suddenly mean we should go back to those days where we lived without technology in the classroom. What it means is that if we want to increase the effect size of technology use in the classroom, we need to couple it with strategies we know from Hattie's research make a difference, namely coaching and feedback. We need someone on staff who provides the perfect balance between understanding how digital devices can be effectively used in instruction and how to pass that understanding on to colleagues through effective professional development. What we need are technology coaches who can create professional development opportunities to make all of this practical for teachers, so they can use it to engage students.

This is where Brad Currie and Emily L. Davis come in. Currie and Davis have vast knowledge and expertise in the areas of technology and coaching. Add that knowledge in with their years of experience and leadership, and we find ourselves with the opportunity to learn from experts how to finally help leverage Hattie's research on the power of coaching to enhance the potential of technology in education. In their new book, *Tech Request: A Guide for Coaching Educators in the Digital World*, Currie and Davis focus on technology coaching, which is an incredibly relevant and important topic for those of us who work in and with schools. Coaching has been researched by so many, and it is always seen as an effective means of providing personalized professional development. Here's the thing though . . . it's only effective when the coach brings a level of credibility and they work with teachers on goals the teachers care about. This book is designed to help anyone tasked with coaching others to integrate technology in their work in a credible and strategic way.

In this book, Currie and Davis build the case for technology coaching. They help educators learn what to do after they get the coaching position and how to create and have an impact on coaching groups. Additionally, one thing I learned deeply from working with Hattie is that we should always be collecting evidence to understand impact, and that's why I find it so important that Currie and Davis have a chapter on gathering and sharing data on the impact of coaching. Equally as important is what coaches can do to stay ahead of the fast-paced world of digital technologies, so Currie and Davis created chapters on staying ahead of the curve, and new world coaching.

Although we have been surrounded by technology for a few decades now, there is still so much to learn about how to utilize it correctly. Part of that process is involving a technology coach who can use their digital expertise in a way that teachers and leaders understand. This book provides more than surface level learning for those who already sit in the digital choir world. Instead, this book is about offering deep and transferable learning to everyone who reads it. Let's see if we can increase the effect size of digital technologies together.

Peter DeWitt, Ed.D.
Author/Consultant
Finding Common Ground blog (*Education Week*)

Introduction

Every student deserves access to an up-to-date education that prepares them for success in all aspects of their life. Understanding how to harness the power of technology to communicate, collaborate, create, and innovate is a necessary skill set in the modern world. In an effort to make this world a reality for students, pre-kindergarten through higher education systems are working to integrate technology into all aspects of education. This is not an easy task as it requires whole systems to fundamentally transform the way they work.

In an attempt to increase technology integration in classrooms, districts, universities, and educational organizations are expending significant funds to purchase technologies. Yet, these resources are often left gathering dust because educators are not yet knowledgeable about how to utilize these new resources. In an attempt to support technology use, organizations are laying out even more resources to hire technology coaches or are using existing staff to take on this important task. While these educators may be proficient in using technology in their own classrooms or settings, learning how to help other educators understand and integrate these tools in their own settings is a challenging task. Further, given the rate at which technology changes, these tech-savvy educators need to understand how to think about technology use more broadly, instead of being experts on one particular tool.

What Do We Mean When We Say Tech Coach?

We use the term, tech coach, to encompass a broad range of roles and responsibilities. Instructional technology coaches are, generally, pre-kindergarten–higher education staff members or others in the educator sector who are tasked with helping other educators understand and integrate technology in their own settings. They may (or may not) have titles such as Technology Coach, Instructional Coach, Program Leader, District or School Leader, or University Faculty Member. Tech coaching may be the full-time role of the educator, or this may be a task that they are asked to take on in addition to or as part of their current roles. These educators are generally proficient in using technology in their own classrooms or settings and are interested in helping others find ways to use it as well.

In sum, anyone tasked with helping educators integrate technology into their practice we consider a tech coach and, therefore, someone who would benefit from reading this book.

This book is for current instructional coaches, technology coaches, those who are interested in becoming an instructional coach, and those who support coaches such as program leaders, school or district administrators, or higher education faculty or staff tasked with helping their colleagues integrate technology into their instruction.

Drawing on the authors' extensive experience in coaching and instructional technology, this book provides research-based and concrete strategies anyone tasked with helping educators integrate technology into their work can use. It explores the role of technology coaches and how they can successfully begin coaching initiatives and unpack strategies for coaching in a variety of common settings including groups and one-to-one coaching. Further, *Tech Request* will help technology coaches and leaders grow their coaching skills, gather data on the impact of their work, overcome challenges, and go deeper. This book includes illustrative vignettes from the field, practical tools, templates, and resources coaches and program leaders can use immediately in their work and ensure the success of their technology coaching initiative. The end goal of this focused work is to enhance educators' effectiveness in using technology to impact teaching and learning at all levels of the system and, ultimately, promote the success of students.

How to Use This Book

This book has been organized as a developmental resource for tech coaches and leaders. If you are new to coaching or running a coaching program, we suggest you begin with Chapter 1 and work through the book in order.

If you have been coaching or leading a tech coaching program for a while, you may want to review the annotated table of contents below and select the chapters and sections that are most critical for you to explore and begin your journey there.

Chapter 1: I'm a Tech Coach ... Now What? Coaches tend to face two significant obstacles at the beginning of a new coaching initiative: 1) Getting clarity on their role from the district or school that hired them, and 2) Recruiting teachers to work with them. This chapter provides guidance, tools, and strategies for helping tech coaches, program leaders, and other stakeholders answer questions such as, "What am I expected to do?", "What outcomes am I expected to produce?", and "What level of confidentiality do I have in my role?" It also provides guidance for explaining coaching to teachers, strategies for building relational trust, and getting a yes from potential coaching clients.

Chapter 2: Tech Coaching 101 Coaching adults requires a different skill set than teaching students. For technology coaches, figuring out how to gauge both emotional and skill readiness in educators, and then help them develop the knowledge and the will to take on new technological innovations, is crucial for success. For those who are new to the art and skill of coaching, or new to coaching around technology, this chapter explores the basics of coaching language and stances, how to tailor coaching to work with teachers at different technology readiness levels, and how to tackle difficult conversations when needed.

Chapter 3: Coaching for Meaningful Technology Integration Technology is intended to be a useful tool educators can use to enhance their pedagogy and improve access to content. Yet, helping teachers to select and use technology meaningfully as part of the instructional process can be challenging. This chapter offers coaches a set of frameworks and a lesson planning tool to guide their thinking and coaching around meaningful tech integration. It also includes resources for helping coaches think about how technology intersects with social-emotional learning, 21st-century skills, and educational equity in planning and instruction. The chapter concludes with ideas for helping educators use technology to connect with parents and further integrate them into the classroom. Coaches walk away ready to guide educators to plan and implement instruction and communication that includes meaningful technology integration.

Chapter 4: Coaching Teams Most technology coaches spend some of their time coaching teams of educators to grow their skill sets. While this may seem like a straightforward task, it can make or break coaches and the initiatives they are attempting to roll out. This chapter includes strategies such as developing norms, maintaining focus, and dealing with questions to help tech coaches carefully plan and facilitate team coaching sessions so that positivity, trust, and willingness to collaborate are fostered while the team makes progress towards its outcomes.

Chapter 5: How's It Going? Gathering and Sharing Data on the Impact of Coaching Most coaching initiatives in schools live and die on their ability to show impact. Therefore, one of the most important—and most overlooked— skills a coach can develop is how to gather, analyze, and share data about the impact of their coaching. This chapter addresses two common questions coaches and coaching programs often ask: "What should we collect?" and "What do we do with what we collect?" by exploring a data collection and impact continuum that coaches, school leaders, and program leaders can use to begin and develop their skills in this critical area. It includes examples of different types of metrics, from simple to more complex, and provides templates coaches can use to gather, analyze, and share their data with a range of stakeholders for both program improvement and sustainability.

Chapter 6: Staying Ahead of the Curve Learning how to keep learning is a crucial role of the coach in a rapidly changing technological world. This chapter focuses on supporting tech coaches to set professional goals utilizing tech coaching standards, making action plans to achieve them, and reflecting on their work as it impacts the broader organization, staff, and students. It also includes strategies and resources tech coaches can use to keep learning including attending conferences, achieving new certifications, school visits, harnessing peer networks, and learning from expert implementers. Readers will walk away with a plan that will truly help them stay ahead of the curve and contribute to their future-ready environments.

Chapter 7: New World Coaching *Tech Request* concludes with a forward look at the range of tech coaching possibilities on the horizon. In just the past few years, tech coaches in many settings have seen their roles grow from supporting the use of individual technologies, infrastructure upgrades, or one-to-one device rollouts, to being tasked with developing STEAM Makerspaces and virtual learning environments, leading robotics and coding initiatives, integrating 3D printers, and computer programming for their district or organization. This shift in focus means that strong technology coaches need to not only be knowledgeable about best practices in teaching, learning, and technology, but also to think beyond any individual tool and consider the broader range of possibilities. The modern-day tech coach must be open-minded and knowledgeable enough to help support the development of learning environments both in the physical and virtual world.

Want more? Connect with us at #TechRequestEDU

1

I'm a Tech Coach . . . Now What?

Gone Are the Days When I Was Just an Instructional Coach

Picture it, a veteran teacher who has taught the same subject in the same classroom for the past 15 years, walks through the front door of school and will no longer walk down the same hallway and sit at the same classroom desk. This year, this veteran teacher is working as an instructional coach. While this is not a new role in schools, the role of instructional coach is changing dramatically. Coaches are now tasked with combining their strong instructional and pedagogical knowledge and skill sets with the world of educational technology.

This new coach will start her day by providing instructional support for a small group of seventh grade teachers as they try and navigate their way through a brand new one-to-one Chromebook initiative. Each teacher is eager, yet apprehensive of how these devices will enhance student learning experiences within their own subject areas. The coach is aware that they are at different comfort and readiness levels when it comes to technology integration and has been thinking about how she will support each of them in the best possible way. She is excited, yet daunted by this undertaking that could ultimately transform the school's learning culture.

How did this role change come about? Towards the end of the previous school year, this veteran teacher approached her administration and spoke about her interest in the newly created instructional technology coach position. The school had made a major investment in Chromebooks the previous year, but found they were not being used consistently across the staff. To support stronger implantation, the school decided to hire an instructional technology coach who could help teachers integrate these new devices in meaningful ways that would enhance their instruction and student learning.

This teacher felt confident in her own education technology use and, over the last several years, the teacher took great pride in being a risk-taker with innovative instructional practices that were well ahead of the times. Now, she was excited about the opportunity of helping her colleagues to also find confidence and success in integrating effective instructional methods with engaging technology use in those same ways.

From an administrative standpoint, appointing this teacher to be the first technology coach in the building was a no-brainer. In addition to her proven skills, she is also well regarded by all school stakeholders. While it was clear they had found the right person for the position, the administrators were unclear about what, exactly, an instructional technology coach would do and how she would be supported in the weeks and months to come. Being a coach of adults is different than teaching students. How will she go about supporting teachers? Should she push into classrooms? Set up appointments? Meet with colleagues before, during, or after school? Will she find success? What does success look like? Would the role support the change they desired? How would she continue to improve as a coach?

As you can tell from this story, coaching can be a fulfilling, yet overwhelming, experience. The questions listed above along with many others consistently arise for both school leaders and instructional coaches from around the globe. Successful coaching is tough work and setting up a coaching program for success requires a lot of careful planning, communication, and implementation to really make it fly.

If you already coach teachers, and are now also being asked to support with technology integration, don't be dismayed. While it is critical to understand technology's role in how students learn and teachers teach, there is no expectation that you will be an expert at every new app or technology that arises. Rather, your job is to coach your colleagues—to listen, to learn alongside them, and to support them in iterating and deepening their practice over time.

This chapter will include critical information coaches and leaders should consider when setting up an instructional technology coaching program. Topics include:

◆ the requisite skills and knowledge effective tech coaches should have;
◆ defining the role of tech coach for all stakeholders; and
◆ how to begin coaching work.

Throughout this chapter, there are concrete tools and strategies for help-ing tech coaches, program leaders, and other stakeholders answer questions such as, "What am I expected to do?", "What outcomes am I expected to produce?", and "What level of confidentiality do I have in my role?" It also provides guidance for explaining coaching to teachers, strategies for building relational trust, and getting a yes from potential coaching clients. The chapter concludes with a checklist to help you get started confidently and smoothly with this new and exciting venture.

What Skills and Knowledge Should a Tech Coach Have?

Like all professional development endeavors, successful instructional technol-ogy coaching programs live or die on the quality of the people who enact them. Through their role, tech coaches directly influence how colleagues perceive the value of the initiative or technology they are working to implement and the professional norms and practices of teachers related to the use of technology. They do so by serving first as models of what successful use of technology can look like—how they think about technology, the way they go about imple-menting it, their attitude when things don't go smoothly, their willingness to network to share ideas and learn from others, and their ability to keep learning in a constantly changing field. You will note we did not say that tech coaches need to be experts in any one particular technology, but rather that they have a way of thinking about technology integration into education that is replicable. So, their own schemas for tech use coupled with their positive and collabora-tive attitude and willingness to help other adults learn mean that they are able to translate their own success into success for others. Successful interactions with tech coaches can positively influence the teacher's own sense of efficacy, and encourage teachers to persevere in implementing current tools as well as increase their willingness to try new tools. Further, technology coaches can also help bring educators together and model new norms of collaboration, curiosity, inquiry, and ongoing learning related to technology that can spread across an entire school or district. This positive, empowered, and professional learning model, coupled with deep expertise from the coach, can reinforce positive attitudes and beliefs about the power of technology in the classroom both for teachers and students. For all of these reasons, it is crucial for program leaders to be very careful about the selection tech coaches in order to ensure the successful implementation of their vision.

One of the first things a school or district needs to consider when building its coaching program is to ensure that the right people are becoming coaches. It is important, therefore, to consider the selection criteria being used to locate potential tech coaches. If you are tasked with finding educators to serve as

Figure 1.1 Top Ten Skills and Dispositions of an Effective Tech Coach

1. Demonstrates success in integrating technology into high-quality instruction.

2. Enjoys building relationships and working collaboratively with others.

3. Personable, positive, and a good communicator.

4. Understands/is interested in adult learning theory.

5. Has a growth mindset: curious, willing to take risks, and a persistent problem-solver.

6. A continuous learner: stays current with best practices in education technology.

7. Leverages networks to enhance effectiveness as a coach.

8. Self-starter: able to figure out new ideas and technologies, best ways to integrate them, and strategies for supporting others in using them.

9. Organized, efficient, self-directed, timely, and able to multitask.

10. Able to lead while, at the same time, taking direction from others.

technology coaches, below is a list of knowledge, skills, and dispositions that you may find helpful in your selection process. Or, if you're already a coach or considering becoming one, consider using this checklist (Figure 1.1) as a tool to self assess your current strengths and areas for growth.

In addition to having the right people in place, there are two key constructs that are critical for new tech coaches—getting role clarity and enrolling coaching clients.

Clarity is Key

Brad is the Director of Planning, Research, and Evaluation for the Chester School District in New Jersey and has worked very closely with the district's six instructional coaches for more than six years. Clarity is very important to him and, because of this, he sets up two monthly meetings with the coaches: one meeting with the technology coaches and one meeting with the literacy and mathematics coaches. The agenda is sent out a week prior to the meeting on a Google Doc and items can be added by Brad or the coaches. During the actual meeting Brad and the coaches will have open and frank conversations about what they are experiencing out in the field.

It's also helpful, and greatly appreciated by the coaches, that Brad shares insight on what he is seeing in the field. Maybe there are certain ways that teachers could enhance their lesson with various forms of technology integration or instructional methods. It's imperative that insights are shared from both sides of the aisle in order to make our great schools even greater. On the same note, it's equally as important for our coaches to reach out to teachers and gauge their insight of how they can help them enhance their effectiveness. Conducting online surveys, attending grade-level or subject area meetings, and having a presence at faculty meetings are some of the ways that helpful information can be collected.

In this vignette, it is clear that both the coaches, the district leader, and the teachers are all quite clear on the roles and responsibilities of the instructional technology coaches. They have a clear scope of work and have support in implementing it as well as continuing to learn and evolve both as individuals as well as members of a strong tech coaching program. Clarity is key.

What is role clarity? A common challenge faced by those tapped to be tech coaches, as well as by those organizing coaching programs, is figuring out what it is instructional tech coaches are expected to do. Each district, school, and institution has a different reason for creating coaching roles. Sometimes coaches are asked to help roll out a specific initiative, system, or technology. In other contexts, coaching is voluntary and coaches must find ways to engage colleagues to work with them. It is critical in both situations to start by getting some clarity on this subject.

In 2015, the Hanover Research Group reviewed the field for best practices in building successful instructional coaching programs and came up with a list of seven key factors in their report, *Best Practices in Instructional Coaching*. We have paraphrased that list here and added some additional information given the unique responsibilities of technology coaches:

1. Establish clear roles and responsibilities for coaches and participants. Successful coaching programs have clear goals. These goals help all stakeholders to make programmatic and resource-related decisions, help coaches focus on the most important activities, and create a clear way to evaluate the success of the program. Further, "clear explanations of teacher, coach, and principal roles helps to set participant expectations and supports the development of trusting, collaborative relationships between teachers and coaches" (p. 4).

    Coming into a tech coaching role, it is critical that coaches ask questions about what the goals of the program are and the scope of their roles. For example, is your role to help a team implement a specific new technology? If so, what does success look like? How are coaches expected to support this implementation? Is there a timeline for implementation? If the answers to questions such as these are not yet established, working with school/district leaders to establish these expectations early will support all stakeholders in experiencing success. Further, if there are other coaches working in the building or district, it is critical to consider early the varying roles of these different people. It is easy for coaches to "overcoach" the same person or to provide mixed messages unintentionally. Discussing with whom each coach might be working, in what capacity, as well as when and how coaches will communicate with each other about what they are doing is also crucially important to establish initially and then ongoing throughout the year.

Once you have defined what the roles and responsibilities of the tech coach are, it can be useful to develop a document or graphic like the one below (Figure 1.2) to support others in

Figure 1.2 What Ed-Tech Coaches Do

Ed-Tech Coaches

Sketchnote by Krista Welz

Introduce new digital tools. Show teachers how they will help instruction & learning.

Work with teachers who are eager to learn and those who are resistant.

Offer professional development that is self-paced, engaging, and choice-based.

Assist in the basic troubleshooting of computers & other digital tools

Helps teachers & administrators become comfortable with technology and assists in the transistion of working with new digital tools & technology

FoLLow ⊙ @KRISTAWELZ

Reproduced by permission of the creator, Krista Welz

understanding what your role is (and is *not*). Having something like this to reference in early meetings with new potential coachees, school leaders, etc. can help ensure everyone is, literally, on the same page from the beginning.

2. Create a system of non-evaluative, respectful adult learning. Coaching adults requires coaches to be able to build trust with those with whom they are working. Without trust, there is generally very little buy-in, risk-taking, or forward movement of practice. Generally, resistance occurs when teachers feel coaches are imposing upon them a system and reporting back to others about their success or failure. Adults learn best when they feel respected, autonomous, and safe.

> Furthermore, because trust and respect are critical for ensuring receptive and meaningful teacher participation, coaches must not be involved in the teacher evaluation process. When coaches act as partners in improving instruction rather than as supervisors or evaluators, teachers will feel more comfortable having open discussions about their practices and taking risks to improve.
>
> (p. 4)

There are some additional considerations that can come up when coaching educators around technology. Generally, people either are comfortable with it, or they aren't. Having space to meet teachers where they are, listen to their needs and challenges, and the leeway to support them in a personalized and appropriate way is crucial for success. Tech coaches need to ask early about to whom they report and what they need to share, the levels of confidentiality around their work with teachers, and how much they can flex to authentically support each coachee. In Chapters 2 and 3, we will unpack the skill sets necessary for coaching adults individually and as a group.

3. Be aware that the coach–principal partnership is critical to programmatic success. Principals and coaches need to work together in order for coaching to succeed. This means that principals need to understand the philosophy of the coaching program, its goals and outcome metrics, and the role of coaches. Being part of the programmatic design team can be helpful in creating this administrative alignment. Further, administrators need to "visibly support" (p. 4) coaching by setting up a coaching culture and participating expectation in their building and clarifying the role of the coach.

Successful tech coaches quickly work to establish relationships with site administrators, find ways to engage or join the instructional leadership team, and set up regular opportunities for learning from those instructional leaders as well as share about what they are doing (in a way that does not break confidentiality with teachers, of course). Generally, technology coaching is work that crosses a variety of established school systems—working one-on-one with teachers, with grade-level or departments, with leadership, and with all staff at times. This means coaches need to quickly get savvy at understanding school-level and district-level systems, where their work fits in, and how best to integrate themselves and their work so that they and the teachers are set up for success.

4. Remember that coaches are instructional leaders . . . but aren't administrators. Coaches and school leaders are both instructional leaders who have the same goal—the success of teachers and students in the building. However, the way in which they go about ensuring this outcome differs. "The principal should remain the school's foremost instructional leader, responsible for the evaluation of teachers and ultimately making final decisions regarding priorities for teaching and learning, while principals and coaches work together toward achieving shared goals for instruction" (p. 4).

Early conversations with school leaders need to be around how the school leader sees technology integration as part of his/her larger vision for the school. What is the school leader's understanding of the outcomes of this work? What does success look like? What are they excited/nervous about? How does the school leader see their role in technology work with the staff? What is the role of the tech coach? Where are their roles the same and where are they different? What processes will the two use to communicate and collaborate to ensure continued alignment? Are there crucial first steps to undertake? Is there a longer-term plan for the year? Multiple years? Knowing at the outset how coaches and school leaders will work together as part of a larger distributed leadership model for the site will help coaches understand their roles while also deepening a critical partnership with site leaders.

5. Make sure resource allocation is appropriate. The most important resource a school or district can give to coaches is time working directly with teachers. There are a few key components to this allocation. First, this means not tasking coaches with other projects or responsibilities. It also means ensuring that they do not have so many teachers on their caseload that they cannot spend enough time with each of them. The literature generally says that a coach–teacher ratio of between 10 and 16 to one is recommended. Finally, teachers need to have time to spend with coaches as well. Making sure that the schedule is set so

that teachers have dedicated time for coaching and can regularly access coaches individually, as part of a group, etc. is critical.

There are lots of ways that this type of resource allocation can be accomplished for tech coaches. As you work with stakeholders to consider goals, success metrics, and your role, the big question to consider is simply how will you organize your time and the teacher's time to best meet your goals? Having clarity on this question will leave you feeling supported and able to achieve the ambitious goals of your new assignment.

6. Prioritize professional development. Learning to coach is hard work. Just because a teacher was great in their own classroom with their own students, or because they love technology, does not mean that they will be great coaches of adults. Coaches need ongoing, high-quality professional development throughout their time as coaches in order to be successful. Coaches' professional learning should include topics such as "practices for teaching adult learners, developing communication skills, and deepening expertise in instructional strategies" (p. 4). Further, coaches need time with one another to make meaning, resolve challenges, and deepen their practice as part of a professional learning community.

It is our hope that your program has a clear, ongoing, and high-quality professional learning plan for you and all the other coaches in your district to learn the basics of coaching adults. As a tech coach, there is additional learning that you need for your role that will support you in keeping abreast of what is going on in a rapidly changing field as well as how to support others in integrating tech into their work (See Chapters 6 and 7 for more ideas on this topic). If there is not yet a plan in place, this is a great place to start with your program leaders to consider how you will keep growing your skills for the benefit of all with whom you work.

7. Make sure your coaching program engages in Continuous Improvement. Connected with the development of goals (listed above in number one), successful coaching programs engage in ongoing programmatic improvement cycles by gathering data, evaluating progress towards clear outcomes, documenting benefits of coaching, identifying areas for improvement, and making strategic changes. There is clear data in the research that high-quality instructional coaching improves teacher and student outcomes, and programs should gather such data about their own programs.

The American Productivity and Quality Center recommends tracking factors related to student achievement, other student outcomes such as discipline and attendance, teacher outcomes such as attrition and retention, and operational factors such as the number of coaching participants and costs.

(p. 5)

In Chapter 5, we will explore a schema for deciding what data to collect and how to collect it in order to best support you in understanding the impact of your work and considering how to use this data to improve outcomes as well as keep your program running and funded! As you begin your work, talking with program leaders about their metrics for success and considering what you might be able to reasonably collect from the beginning will go a long way to getting you off in the best possible manner.

Coaching is a complex process and there are many key pieces required to make it successful. Having role clarity as a new tech coach requires you to understand how each of the seven components described above is being addressed in your coaching situation. Below is a list of questions (Figure 1.3) to ask that should support you in figuring out what, exactly, you have been tapped to do:

Figure 1.3 Gaining Coaching Role Clarity Questionnaire

1. **Establish clear roles and responsibilities for coaches and participants.**
   - What am I expected to do in my role? Is there a specific initiative I am being tapped to implement?
   - What should my day/week look like?
   - What am I expected to produce as part of my work?
2. **Create a system of non-evaluative, respectful adult learning.**
   - What level of confidentiality do I have in my work with teachers?
   - What expectations are there that teachers will work with me? (i.e. Are they required to work with me or am I responsible for recruiting volunteers?)
   - How have my role and expectations about coaching been conveyed to teachers?
   - How will we talk with others in our organization about my role?
3. **The coach–principal partnership is critical to programmatic success.**
   - How do site administrators see coaches in their buildings?
   - How often will coaches and site administrators meet?
   - What am I expected to share with administrators about my work?
4. **Coaches are instructional leaders . . . but aren't administrators.**
   - What is the school leader's understanding of the outcomes of this work?
   - What are they excited/nervous about?
   - How does the school leader see their role in technology work with the staff?
   - What is the role of the tech coach?
   - Where are their roles the same and where are they different?
   - What processes will we use to communicate/collaborate to ensure continued alignment?
   - Are there crucial first steps to undertake?
   - Is there a longer-term plan for the year? Multiple years?

5. **Appropriate resource allocation is crucial.**
   - How many teachers will I work with? In what formats?
   - What time is available for me to work with teachers or groups of teachers?
   - What resources are available to support me in my work with teachers?

6. **Coaches need to be intentionally developed.**
   - What kind of initial and ongoing support will I have to learn how to make the most of my role?
   - How often do coaches meet for ongoing learning?
   - What resources and/or supports are in place to help me continue to learn about my unique role as a tech coach?

7. **Engage in Continuous Improvement.**
   - What does success look like?
   - What data should I/the program collect to help me/us understand whether we are meeting our goals? How will we analyze that data for the purposes of ongoing learning?
   - Is there a timeline for implementation/meeting these success criteria?
   - How is data shared with other key stakeholders?
   - How will I be evaluated? By whom?
   - How will the coaching program be evaluated? By whom?

We encourage you to spend some time asking the questions that will support you and others in getting clarity about your role. Be thoughtful, particularly as you work with others to get clear about how your role is shared with others—particularly teachers. How you are introduced to them will have a lasting impact on how willing they are to work with you.

How Do I Land My First Recruits?

Once you've gotten some clarity on your role, it is time to get out there and start coaching! So, how do you do that? Slow and low is a method that can be used by an instructional coach as they initially attempt to make an impact on how teachers leverage the power of technology. Particularly if the coach is new to a school or district it will be critical that they first get to know the staff, build on those initial relationships, and then demonstrate that they can have an impact on instruction and learning. Coaches need to get colleagues excited about the possibility of working with them and the positive impact it could have on teachers and on their students. Obviously it helps if the coach has a previous working relationship with the colleagues they are going to assist, but sometimes this is not the case. In all honesty, educators do not like it when things are shoved down their throats. There needs to be a purpose behind every tool and methodology. To that end, most educators appreciate the support they receive over an extended period of time, but that is also beneficial in a way that whatever they are exposed to can be implemented in the immediate future. So how do you land your initial recruits as an instructional coach who is tasked with finding unique ways to integrate technology? Build relational trust, establish confidentiality, and provide assistance in a timely fashion. These three initial steps will help you begin the process of enrolling coaching clients and get you started on your work together. Let's unpack each of these concepts in turn.

1. Build Relational Trust

The single most important thing a new coach can do is work intentionally to build relational trust with colleagues. Rafael Echeverria and Julio Olalla stated it the most clearly, "Without trust there can be no coaching" (1993). What is relational trust? Annette Baier writes, "We inhabit a climate of trust as we inhabit an atmosphere and notice it as we notice air, only when it becomes scarce or polluted" (1994, p. 98). Researchers Bryk and Schneider who studied Chicago schools, found that when schools had strong levels of trust as they began change efforts, they were twice as likely to improve reading and math achievement, as opposed to a one in seven chance of making gains where trust was weak (2003). These studies point to the fact that when educators trust one another, they are more willing to be honest, work together, take risks, and improve. Coaching requires participants to feel vulnerable in front of others, to take risks, to struggle, and even to fail. No one is willing to be this open with someone whom they do not trust. Bottom line? Trust matters.

It's also important to know that there are intentional moves coaches can make that lead to the development and maintenance of trust in schools. In her article, "Trust Matters", Valerie Von Frank (2010), describes five elements of trust that were laid out by researchers Wayne Hoy and Megan Tschannen-Moran (2003):

1. Benevolence: Confidence that one's well-being or something one cares about will be protected by the trusted party . . . the assurance that others will not exploit one's vulnerability or take advantage even when the opportunity is available. The cost of the absence of benevolence is productivity, they say, because people spend their energy thinking about and planning for alternatives.
2. Honesty: The trusted person's character, integrity, and authenticity . . . acceptance of responsibility for one's actions and not distorting the truth in order to shift blame to another. Any dishonesty breaches trust and breeds further distrust.
3. Openness: The extent to which relevant information is shared . . . openness signals reciprocal trust. When leaders are not open, staff become suspicious and wonder what is being hidden and why. Rumors drive people's actions in a negative way.

4. Reliability: Consistency of behavior and knowing what to expect from others . . . a sense of confidence that one's needs will be met in positive ways. Without a sense of a leader's reliability, people spend their energy worrying about whether they will be supported and making mental provisions for not being so. Reliability often involves the skill of time management for leaders, Tschannen-Moran said.

5. Competency: The ability to perform as expected and according to standards appropriate to the task at hand. Trust can be limited no matter how someone perceives the other's benevolence, reliability, openness, and honesty if the other person does not have the requisite skill and knowledge, for example, as a teacher.

Similarly, in her TED Talk, social scientist, Brené Brown, describes seven elements that makes us trust others and ourselves.

1. Boundaries: We respect each others boundaries. When we are not clear about what's okay and not okay, we ask. It's okay to say no.

2. Reliability: We do what we say we will do. We are aware of our competencies and limits. We don't over promise and are able to deliver on commitments.

3. Accountability: Mistakes happen. When they do, we own them, apologize, and make amends.

4. Vault: We keep what happens between us private and don't share anything that is not ours to share.

5. Integrity: We choose what is right over what is fun, fast, or easy. We practice our values rather than just professing them.

6. Non-Judgment: We can talk honestly without fear of being judged and and can ask for what we need.

7. Generosity: We hold positive presuppositions about each other's intentions, words, and actions. We assume people want to do their best and are acting from that place.

She uses the acronym BRAVING to remember these.

These two lists include a lot of similar elements. At their core are a few key actions coaches can take that are more likely to build relational trust and help maintain it throughout your work together. These include: being reliable and accountable, maintaining confidentiality, assuming the best in others, being non-judgmental, and showing competence.

So, how do we build relational trust? Practice active listening. Yes, listening. Most people only actively listen for about 17 seconds before either tuning out or beginning to think about what they want to say in response. Most people state that they rarely feel truly listened to. So, from this perspective, listening is a truly valuable gift that that you can give to someone!

Active listening, therefore, requires the listener to turn off that part of the brain that is waiting for the other person to take a breath so you can say what you want to say and, instead, listen to truly understand what the other person is saying. The listener must pay attention—not only to the speaker, but to themselves—to their frame of mind as well as their body language in order to ensure they are listening respectfully, without judgment or criticism, and are truly present in the moment. You will know you are doing it right when you have to pause after the other person is done speaking so you can formulate a response.

Active listeners practice *reflecting* back what they are hearing from the other person—both their information as well as their emotions—by paraphrasing (not parrot-phrasing) key points. Paraphrasing is a key strategy to ensure the listener truly understands what the speaker is saying instead of assuming they understood. It helps the speaker know you are on the same page and that you really "get" what they are saying.

Active listeners also work to *clarify* their understanding by encouraging the speaker to expand upon their ideas and reflect on their thinking by asking open-ended and probing questions that help both the listener and speaker to refine their ideas and understanding. Clarifying requires the listener to work from a stance of genuine curiosity instead of judgment or a desire to lead the speaker to any particular outcome.

Active listeners also help the speakers to see larger themes in the conversation and share these with the speaker by *summarizing, making connections between ideas, and supporting the speaker in developing a schema* for thinking about the topic in a broader way.

Active listening gives you, as a coach, a clearer understanding of the other person's perspective, knowledge, and needs. It allows us to search for natural *entry points*—places where the speaker is either at the edge of their knowledge or may need assistance—and determine what we may want to offer that will fit their needs. Searching for entry points through active listening means that the speaker not only feels really heard by you, but also is more willing to work with you because you have offered something you are sure they need. Doing so builds trust quickly as well as buy-in for ongoing work together.

Coaching is not just a technical application of tools, but rather an agreement between people to really work together for a greater good. Nothing truly will happen until trust is fully established.

2. Establish Confidentiality

Earlier in this chapter, while unpacking role clarity, we discussed the importance of understanding the levels of confidentiality you have in both your work with teachers as well as with administrators. Teachers also need to be clear about how much you will share about your work together and with whom you will share it. Truly effective coaching needs to be confidential in nature. It is an integral part of building relational trust. We also cannot stress enough that if you say you are going to be confidential, then you really need to make sure you follow through on that agreement. If you violate a teacher's confidentiality, it will be very hard, if not impossible, to regain their trust. It is also important to note here that you may have to repeat this confidentiality agreement over and over again, especially at the beginning, before teachers will fully believe you. This may be so particularly in cases where a teacher has previously had interactions with a coach that were not confidential or in which their confidentiality was violated.

We also know that you have a working relationship with site administrators and others as part of the instructional leadership team. You are all working towards the same goal—success of the coaching initiative, teachers, and students—and you will talk with them regularly about your work. The challenge for a coach is to engage in those conversations without violating the confidentiality of the teachers whom you are coaching. Here are a few moves that Emily teaches coaches which may be helpful on this front:

1. Reassure teachers that, even though you talk regularly with administrators, you aren't sharing the details of your work with them. If there is something you would like to share, or something you think the teacher should share, you will talk to the teacher about it first.

2. Be very clear with administrators from the beginning that your work with teachers is confidential and that you won't share specifics of their work. However, your goal is to work in alignment with the site administrator to meet their goals and you are anxious to hear their impressions and thoughts about what is working and not so you can adjust your coaching to help teachers achieve.

3. Don't make evaluative statements. When a well-meaning administrator asks you directly about a teacher whom you are coaching, try turning the question around by stating something like, "Thanks for asking. I am wondering if you could share your perceptions of how the teacher is doing. This would really help me to ensure that I am coaching this teacher in ways that align with your vision of success."

4. Joellen Killion and Cindy Harrison (2006) also suggest that coaches might be able to *share the four Ts with administrators: teacher, time, topics, and tasks*. They can share the teachers with whom they are working, how much time is spent with a coachee, the broad topics of work—hopefully ones that are in alignment with the teacher's

Figure 1.4 Coaching Log Example

Teacher	Date/Time	Topics	Tasks
Ms. G	2/2/18, 3rd period	Ongoing formative assessment	Using Google Forms to drive real-time feedback
Mr. C	2/3/18, 5th period	Student voice	Integrating Flipgrid and Qball to promote student's voice

and administrator's common goals, and tasks the coach is doing with the coachee such as observing, looking at student work, etc. As a note of caution here, coaches must ensure that when they disclose this information with administrators, that it is shared only in non-evaluative ways. Sometimes setting up formal processes for sharing this information, such as through a coaching log that the coach, teacher, and site administrator all see, can support both the non-evaluative nature of the sharing as well as demonstrating to the teacher how you are maintaining confidentiality. Figure 1.4 is an example of such a log.

For coaching to be truly effective, teachers need to feel that they can be open and vulnerable with you without repercussions. Establishing confidentiality early and reinforcing it often both with the teacher and the administrator will go a long way to ensuring your coaching work starts and continues successfully.

3. Provide Assistance in a Timely Fashion

Before there were wonderful tech coaches in his current district, Brad would often be the one of the chosen few to support staff as they looked to integrate various forms of technology in their classroom. Whether it was using the Smartboard, leveraging G Suite for Education, understanding the impact of a new web application, or unpacking the latest real-time assessment tool, it was imperative that Brad understood the teacher's instructional need and then planned how best to support a particular colleague in meaningful and timely fashion. His philosophy on helping educators with technology has always been, "The longer they wait, the less likely they will initiate." If teacher came to Brad with an idea on how to integrate a new online program, he knew he better research it thoroughly and come up with a game plan quickly so the teacher could see it in action before they lost momentum. If Brad put off his colleagues for even a few weeks, there was a strong likelihood that they would lose interest and never come back.

The impetus behind this book is based on the reality that there are thousands of websites, apps, and devices that could potentially be used by a teacher, student, or administrator. Now more than ever, educators need a support structure in place that will help with navigating the digital world in an effective and innovative fashion. We must always remember that a student's job is to learn, a teacher's job is to teach, and a leader's job is to lead. So whatever we can do to make their jobs easier, it is the job of coaches to do so.

As we mentioned before, part of building a trusting relationship is doing what you say you will do when you said you will do it. If teachers see that you are, indeed, helpful, they are more likely to continue to work with you over time. If we have engaged in active listening and really listened to understand what a teacher might need, we may have heard an entry point on which we can capitalize as a coach.

Ask Permission to Coach

Before we jump in and begin making suggestions, it is critical that we *ask for permission to coach*. We can say things such as, "Are you interested in hearing some ideas that might be helpful in this situation?" or "I am hearing your challenge around implementation. Might you be open to having me come and observe next time you are trying this? It might help us figure out our next steps together." Whether we like it or not, there is an unspoken power dynamic between teachers and coaches. You have a "fancy" title and, therefore, must have some additional authority. Asking permission to coach can break down the power dynamic by allowing the teacher to remain in control of the situation and choose how they would like to proceed. Further, it demonstrates the coaches' genuine respect for the teacher as a fellow professional and their interest in genuine collaboration.

Follow Through

Once a teacher has assented to working with you, it is critical that *you do what you say you will do*. If you say you will provide a resource, do so. If you say you will come and observe, show up. If you say you are collecting data on how students are using a device, do that. It is very easy to overcommit as a coach—to take on more than we can do well, to foreshorten deadlines, and to overpromise on outcomes. New tech coaches will do well to heed the warning to underpromise and overdeliver. By regularly keeping our commitments, we demonstrate our usefulness as coaches and increase the likelihood we will be asked back to do more coaching.

The role of an instructional coach in the digital era is critical and, quite frankly, a necessity to a school's culture of learning. The amount of money, time, and resources that support teaching and learning through technology can no longer be overlooked. Instructional coaches across all disciplines must enhance their knowledge of how technology can impact educational environments. So much so, that the Future Ready Schools initiative created a framework for instructional coaches to guide the important work they do as change agents.[1] Throughout this book we will connect you, the reader, with insights, ideas, strategies, and resources that will help support your efforts as an innovative instructional coach.

Putting It All Together

In this chapter, we have unpacked three critical concepts: 1) Understanding what knowledge and skills are necessary to be an effective instructional technology coach, 2) Getting clarity on the roles and responsibilities of the coach for all stakeholders, and 3) Getting started enrolling teachers in coaching work. The next chapter in this book will explore the coaching tools you need to really get started supporting teachers as they work to better integrate technology into their practice.

Note

1 You can access it here: http://1gu04j2l2i9n1b0wor2zmgua-wpengine.netdna-ssl.com/wp-content/uploads/2017/07/Instructional_coaches_flyer.pdf.

References

Baier, A. (1994). *Moral Prejudices: Essays on Ethics.* Cambridge, MA: Harvard University 1994.

Brown, B. (June 2010). "The Power of Vulnerability." Speech at TEDx Houston. Retrieved from: www.ted.com/talks/brene_brown_on_vulnerability.

Bryk, A.S. & Schneider, B. (2003). Trust in schools: A core resource for school reform. *Educational Leadership*, 60(6), 40–45.

Echeverria, R. & Olalla, J. (1993). *The Art of Ontological Coaching.* Boulder, CO: Newfield Network.

Hanover Research Group. (December 2015). *Best Practices in Instructional Coaching.* Prepared for the Area Education Agencies. Retrieved from: www.esc5.k12.in.us/index.php/inside-wvec/documents-and-forms/

resources-for-instructional-coaches/856-best-practices-in-instructional-coaching-iowa-area-education-agencies-1/file.

Hoy, W.K. & Tschannen-Moran, M. (2003). The conceptualization and measurement of faculty trust in schools. In W. Hoy & C. Miskel (Eds.), *Studies in Leading and Organizing Schools* (pp. 181–208). Greenwich, CT: Information Age Publishing.

Killion, J. & Harrison, C. (2006). *Taking the Lead: New Roles for Teachers and School-Based Coaches*. Oxford, OH: National Staff Development Council.

Von Frank, V. (2010). Trust matters: For educators, parents, and students. *Tools for Schools, 14*(1), 1–8.

2

Tech Coaching 101

Two pieces of advice I would give to a technology coach. First, where there is a will there's a way. Whenever a teacher asks if a program can do something or if they are looking for a way for their students to learn a skill using digital tools, I always start with YES, sure, of course we can. Just having the hope that there can be an answer to the question drives both of us to a positive place. Sometimes we need to think outside the box or ask more experts on a topic but we keep looking for the answer. 98% of the time we find a way but the process always starts with ... YES we can!

My second piece of advice is less about the technology and more about the person. Be approachable about anything! I have learned that everyone has a story. Sometimes in order to work with them, we need to know their story. I have been tempted to feel like ... "Don't they know I am busy" or "I am here for the tech question not a personal narrative." I have to take a deep breath and learn to care about the whole person and not just their tech question. When I do, magic happens. They are able to articulate their question and we can get to the bottom of the need. Then I refer to what I mentioned above, "Of course, we can figure that out. Where there's a will, there's a way!" We both walk away feeling as though it was a positive experience which leads to more questions and repeat customers.

Laura Garrison, Technology Coach,
Chester School District in Chester, New Jersey

In the last chapter, we focused in on how tech coaches can develop clarity about their role, what is expected of them, and how to begin developing the critical relationships with teachers necessary to work together on new initiatives. In this chapter, we will turn our attention to how tech coaches can achieve their coaching goals. We will unpack practical strategies for:

- understanding teacher strengths and needs;
- how to tailor coaching to best support teachers as individuals; and
- supporting teachers when things aren't going well.

Let's dive in to each of these areas in turn.

Getting Curious: Coaching as Detective Work

It is important for coaches to remember that no two educators are alike. The fact that you experience something in a certain way does not mean that this is also the way your coachees have or will experience it. Each educator has different strengths, needs, interests, and experiences that they bring to any coaching situation. It is the job of the coach, therefore, to learn as much about their coachee or client as possible and to figure out how to build on that person's unique strengths as well as help them address any challenges in the most positive way possible.

The best analogy we have for the way coaches can go about this process of learning about an educator is to employ a detective's mind-set. The job of a detective is to meticulously search for clues, patterns, leads, and connections that help to create a larger picture of the situation. While detectives may have hunches about what is occurring or why, they are slow to make judgments or take action without all the information. They keep searching until their curiosity is satisfied. For a detective, jumping to conclusions or action too soon can have precipitous consequences.

Coaches must operate in a similar fashion. It is natural to make quick judgments based on our experiences, but we must, instead, slow down and carefully take stock of what is actually going on before we move to action. Like a detective, we search for clues in an educator's words and actions that help us know more about what they know and don't know, what they value and what they detest, what gets them motivated and what has the opposite effect. Slowly, through conversation, interactions, and observation, we create a picture of this person.

There are limits to the detective analogy, however. Whereas detectives seek to find guilt, coaches seek to find and enhance the best in those with whom they interact. A critical underlying assumption of good coaching is

Positive Presupposition. We define positive presupposition as the belief that each of us is doing the best we can with what we know and what we have in our tool kits. We are not aiming to be mediocre or bad at something, if we are not expert at it yet, it may be because we do not yet have what we need to succeed. This stance is critical to take because it helps coaches to move from a natural stance of judging what we see to viewing it with a sense of curiosity. Instead of thinking, "Wow, I would never do that in my classroom," coaches with positive presupposition reframe their thinking as, "I wonder what is going on here. I am curious about the moves this teacher is making and what she hopes to accomplish. I need to find out more." This seemingly simple move has big implications for coaching success. It allows coaches to move from an oppositional stance—I am going to tell you what is wrong and how to fix it—to a collaborative stance—how can we work together to make this even better?

Assuming that a teacher wants to be excellent, that they do have strengths and skills on which to build, and believing that together you can achieve great things is a foundational mind-set for successful coaching. If tech coaches can train themselves to approach all situations in this way, they will be more likely to set themselves and their clients up for successful work together.

Formatively Assessing Teacher Will and Skill

So, what are technology coaches looking for that will help them know more about a coachee?

Our favorite framework for thinking about an educator's readiness to work with a coach is the will/skill matrix. First made popular by Max Landsberg in the *Tao of Coaching* (1996), a coach asks him/herself two basic questions about any person:

1. How much does the person really want to complete the task? (Will)
2. How much can this person rely on his/her skill to complete the task? (Skill)

Landsberg and others have created matrices that help coaches to formatively group teachers into one of four archetypes (Figure 2.1).

We specifically call these categories archetypes because no one is ever in any one of these categories all of the time in all situations. We all have the potential to be in any of these categories based on the situation. For example, Emily is often quite high willed and high skilled when it comes to learning something new at yoga, but is much lower skilled and lower

what is a small win? (handwritten)

Figure 2.1 Will-Skill Matrix

add Knowledge (handwritten)

add attention to avoid more failure (handwritten)

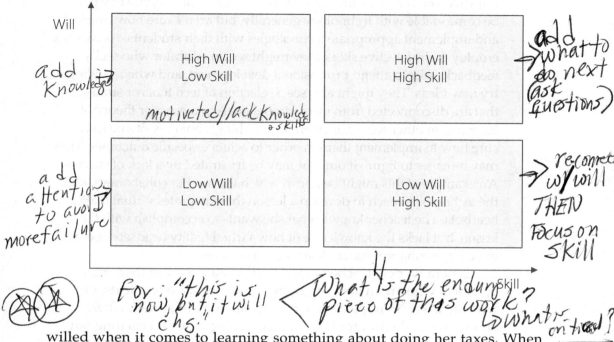

High Will Low Skill *motiveted/lack Knowledge & skills* (handwritten)	High Will High Skill
Low Will Low Skill	Low Will High Skill

add what to do next (ask questions) (handwritten)

reconned w/ will THEN Focus on Skill (handwritten)

for: "this is now, but it will chg." (handwritten)

What is the enduring piece of this work? (handwritten)

what's on trad? (handwritten)

willed when it comes to learning something about doing her taxes. When we throw technology into the mix, it can complicate things further for coaches and the people they are coaching. Generally, educators (and all people) have pretty strong feelings about technology. Some are quite comfortable, easily pick up new tech, and feel confident they can resolve any problems should they arise. On the other end of the spectrum are folks who, for a variety of reasons, distrust or are uncomfortable with technology. These folks require convincing and ongoing support to implement something new. Any new challenges feel significant for such users and can create serious setbacks to implementation.

Even if we have a sense that a coachee feels a certain way about technology overall, our goal as tech coaches must be to avoid pigeonholing a coachee into any particular quadrant described above and assume that will always be the way they are related to technology. Rather, the goal is to stay curious and formatively assess where a coachee is in a particular situation and/or with a piece of technology. Then, using that assessment, make decisions about the most effective coaching strategy for this encounter. Next time you meet with that teacher, you will need to reassess the situation and adjust your plan accordingly.

Our favorite resource for using this matrix to coach educators comes from Robyn Jackson's book, *Never Underestimate Your Teachers* (2013). Below, we've adapted Jackson's four archetypal descriptions to consider coachee's comfort with technology and the tech coaching moves that might be useful:

Robin Jackson (handwritten)
Never Underestimate Your Teach (handwritten)

1. *High Will, Low Skill.* These educators are really motivated and want to improve, but may lack the knowledge or skills to do so yet. They may be comfortable with technology generally, but aren't sure how to select and implement appropriate technologies with their students. As coaches employ their detective skills, they might see an educator who seeks feedback, asks to attend professional development, and who is willing to try new ideas. They might also see a selection of tech tools or strategies that are disconnected from instructional goals or a broader theory of teaching. In other words, they are trying things, but may not be fully sure how to implement them in order to achieve specific outcomes. They may be eager to figure it out, but may be frustrated by a lack of success. An example of this might be one in which the teacher collaborates with the technology coach to develop a lesson that integrates virtual reality headsets. The teacher knows what she wants to accomplish with the lesson, but lacks the knowledge of how virtual reality headsets operate in order to enhance student learning experiences.

    Generally, new teachers fall into this category, but there may be others who are in new situations, grade levels, or contexts, or who are asked to implement a new technology or system where an experienced educator is facing something new and exciting but hasn't yet figured out what works in this situation. With a coaching focus on supporting skill development, this educator will really fly.

    A quick coaching word of caution, while the focus should primarily be on knowledge and skill development (i.e. How do we select an application that will best meet your instructional goals? Or, how do we introduce this kind of a system to students?), it is important to continue to pay attention to their will. Repeated failure and/or lack of progress can begin to impact even the most high-willed individual. Make sure you continue to support them in seeing progress and growth even when it feels slow or frustrating.

2. *Low Will, Low Skill.* Educators who fall into this category may look as if they have given up because they seem to be missing key skills and don't seem to be interested in improving. Coaches might see clues such as a teacher only doing the bare minimum required (i.e. the tech only comes out when the principal is in the room), not volunteering ideas or information, dismissing data, and waving off offers of assistance for implementation help from coaches and others. For example, the math coach in the district rolls out an online benchmark assessment program that provides students and parents with real-time information to help identify gaps with solving problems. A few teachers refuse to learn about and implement the program stating that they prefer paper and pencil assessments.

Frankly, these are the educators that make most coaches shake their heads in frustration. It is important to remember, however, that there are many reasons why low will and low skill might occur situationally. For example, these might be folks who, at one point, were more willing to try out new systems or technologies but, after repeated failure due to a lack of knowledge or skill, are less willing to engage now. Being asked to do something you have never done with no training and having it go badly day after day can break the will of even the most dedicated educator. The coaches' job, therefore, is to get curious about what drives or "wakes up" this educator. Is it low will that needs to be addressed first? (i.e. What got this person excited about introducing tech in the first place? What problem might a specific application solve? What is it they wish could be automated to make life easier for them in their classrooms?). Or does the lack of skill need to be addressed first? (i.e. Where are they being repeatedly unsuccessful that is causing the frustration? What small but meaningful changes can be made quickly that will get them back on the road to success?)

As a word of caution, these are folks who may need their coach to sit side-by-side with them and walk through each step, who may need to see explicit modeling and/or engage in co-teaching to help build their will along with their skill. If they struggle, they need direct support in how to find and access resources to overcome an obstacle so that they do not need to rely only on the coach to resolve situations. Coaches must be careful not to create overreliance on themselves. They must consider what will happen when they are no longer available to support their colleague. They need to ensure the coachee can be successful long after they leave the scene.

3. *Low Will, High Skill.* These teachers have the knowledge and skills necessary to be excellent, but may not be interested in improving for some reason. Coaches may see technology being utilized mainly as a replacement for paper and pencil tasks, or see a comfort with the technology they use already, along with an understanding of how the applications connect with their outcomes. They may also notice that this colleague is less interested in learning anything new or considering how to take the technology they are using from replacement to enhancement of learning. They may have a strongly positive view of their own practice and not be open to feedback that highlights areas for improvement. They may resist new programs or curricula and encourage others to resist it as well. There is an overall sense of, "It is just fine the way it is." This might look like a tech savvy science teacher who completely understands how to utilize

and integrate technology, but he will only develop innovative lesson plans when he knows the principal is coming in for evaluation purposes. Constant recommendations to collaborate with technology coaches are for the most part ignored.

Generally, these educators were historically high will, high skill with technology, but something frustrating or disappointing happened that left them less than willing to engage again. If a coach notices these signs in a potential coachee, it is critical to get curious about that past disappointment and focus on how to help them reconnect with their will so they can return to that highly functional place once more. What have they found useful about the technological solutions they are currently using? What more would they like to do? Thinking about small wins that help improve the quality of their work and get them excited again about trying new things is an important step to take to getting these folks back on the road to high will and high skill.

4. *High Will, High Skill.* From the moment you step into the classrooms of these teachers, it is clear you are in presence of a master educator. They are clearly motivated to help all students succeed, have strong pedagogical and content knowledge, understand and can articulate why they do what they do, and are interested in continuing to learn and grow. They have considered how to use technology to not just replace something that was originally done using paper and pencil, but instead to enhance their practice and student learning.

At a building-wide level, this might look like the building principal leveraging the power of social media to inform stakeholders and highlight student and staff achievements. The coaches worked with the principal to set up the Twitter feed and other social media venues, determine how to curate these feeds, and problem-solve any situations that arise. On a daily basis the principal tweets out pictures of classroom learning experiences and extracurricular activities and the technology coaches in the building support the principal by helping to run the various social media accounts.

Often, these educators are overlooked for coaching in schools because there are other more pressing situations in a building to which coaches are deployed or coaches hesitate to offer suggestions to those they deem masters. Master teachers, however, can benefit from coaching as much as everyone else. Without new challenges, high-will, high-skill teachers can grow bored or frustrated (i.e. high-skill, low-will teachers) or they may choose to leave teaching altogether. The kind of coaching they need, however, is different. They need acknowledgement of the things they are doing well, conversations that explore nuance of technological usage to enhance instruction, and support taking on new tech tools of interest to them. With this kind of support, these educators continue to grow and adapt as technologically savvy master educators.

Determining what might support a teacher in moving forward—whether support focused on will or skill (or both!)—is a great place to start to tailor your coaching work to meet the needs of the educators with whom you have the opportunity to work. How you go about doing that work is the next opportunity for tailoring the next step.

Taking a HUMAN Approach

Once we have formatively diagnosed where a teacher might be today in their will and skill, we need to figure out how best to respond to them. Brad says that we need to take a HUMAN approach to coaching (Figure 2.2):

More than anything else, people appreciate other people who are **human-like**. Seems pretty simple right? Unfortunately, the human side of things gets lost in the mix. For the most part, colleagues approach their instructional coach because they have set some sort of goal, no matter how small or big, that they want to attain. And often, technology enters into the equation which means that there could be some minor glitches along the way. People sometimes become frazzled when technology does not work the way they want it to and act a bit out of sorts when relaying frustration to the person who is providing support. It's important to take advantage of this opportunity and assure the person that the situation will be resolved. Eye contact, a calming demeanor, and relaying the specific plan of attack are all important elements in helping the person with the glitches they are encountering in trying to achieve their goal. The hardest thing to do sometimes as a coach who is supporting their colleague with integrating technology is keeping emotions in check. Once the situation is addressed, your colleague will remember two things: how you helped them out and the way in which you helped them out.

Figure 2.2 HUMAN Approach

H—Be humanlike, connect with colleagues, and show them that reaching a goal is possible.
U—Understand the situation and issues identified by your colleagues.
M—Manage the situation and people involved with dignity .
A—Attain the goal you set to the address situation by exhausting all options.
N—Never give up! Stay connected and follow up after goal is reached.

Understanding the current situation and issues presented to you by your colleague is an incredibly important quality of a coach. Working with people of various abilities can prove challenging but will keep things interesting for sure. At one point during the day you could be helping someone with learning how to set up their classroom website and at a later point team teaching with a colleague as a way to offer support as the class uses an online video editor program for an upcoming project. Understanding what your colleagues are capable of technology-wise connects closely with the relationship you have formed with them over time. Truly gaining a grasp on what your fellow educator is capable of could potentially take months or even years. Staying the course and letting them know that you have their back will push them to be more confident and take risks in order to promote the success of students.

Managing the situations and people you interact with can only be done in one way and that's in a dignified manner. Humans can be tough cookies from time to time and are dealing with real-life issues inside and outside of school. Working with and supporting folks in good times and bad is without a doubt one of the toughest responsibilities that a coach must handle. Remaining calm, organized, and unflappable can go a long way. But make no mistake about it, even coaches can have bad days. And if it happens? Own up to it! Apologize, explain, and make things right in a timely fashion. Who knows, a colleague that you are supporting may conduct themselves in the same fashion if they are having an off day.

Attaining the goal you set for yourself and your colleague is easier said than done. Say, for example, your vice principal approached you about coordinating a Parent Tech Night. Kind of a big deal right? Exhausting all options to make this night a huge success is a huge undertaking. What do you want the parents to learn? How many sessions should there be? Which colleagues do you reach out to? Once your goals are established and a plan is created it's now just a matter of following through. Reaching out to some of your colleagues that you have helped in the past is a good starting point. They will want to contribute to this great night of learning for the parents of their students. Participating in this sort of experience will validate everything they have done in terms of working with you as a coach. It's always a good thing to connect with parents and help them see what you see as it relates to the power of technology.

Never give up when trying to reach your own goals or the goals of others. It's important to understand that helping your fellow colleagues doesn't happen in just one sitting. It could days, weeks, or even months. Stay in constant contact with them by dropping by, informally observing, text messaging, or email. They should know that you mean business and that no matter what is going on in your world they are always one of your top priorities. If a tool or strategy doesn't work, go back to the drawing board and find the solution they are looking for.

Taking the **HUMAN** approach can be very beneficial for tech ̣
as they look to make an impact on their fellow colleagues' ability to
students through technology. This positive approach will quickly help
ers see you as not only a knowledgeable colleague, but one who will provide
valuable support with their best interest in mind.

Words Matter: Coaching for Autonomy and Change

The way we talk with those we are coaching is just as important, if not more
so, than what we are talking about with them. The language and stances
coaches use—the way they organize coaching conversations, ask questions,
and offer ideas—is a critical tool set for any coach to master. As we discussed
in the last chapter, it can be easy for a coach to listen to or watch a teacher at
work, instantly judge their practice, and quickly move to offering solutions
to the perceived issue. Instead, we need to assume that the teacher (especially
a more veteran one) has much of what she already needs to resolve her own
situation and that our job is to help her use her own knowledge and skills to
get there. We do so by helping to organize the conversation in a productive
way, keep track of and illuminate thinking, and, if invited to do so, offer ideas
or options based on our experience. What we do not want is for a teacher to
come to depend upon the coach to solve all her problems. Instead, what we
want is to help the teacher develop or refine thinking and planning processes
so that, when faced with similar situations in the future, she has everything
she needs to resolve the situation successfully and independently. So what
does coaching for autonomy and change look like? It will be different for each
teacher with whom we work. However, there are some flexible tools that
coaches can use to help organize the coaching conversation.

One framework we like to use is the Instructive-Collaborative-Facilitative
(I-C-F) Framework first developed by Carl Glickman (2002). Many coaching organizations, including New Teacher Center, use this framework as the
basis for thinking about how coaches can adapt to meet the needs of teachers.
The big idea here is that not all teachers need the same level of support from a
coach. There is a continuum of support that a coach can offer. Effective coaching matches the knowledge and needs of the teacher with whom the coach is
working. Let's consider what this looks like from a tech coaching perspective:

- *Instructive Stance*. When it is clear a teacher is at the edge of their
  knowledge or skill and needs information, ideas, or direction, a
  coach might provide instructive coaching support. In this stance,
  the coach directs the interaction based on assessed needs, provides
  information, and offers suggestions and solutions with rationale.

there is a coach provider hole - invitation to do something new

Examples of instructive coaching might include sharing a process for implementing a new technology tool with students, modeling an instructional technology for a teacher, or suggesting a strategy for using technology to look at student data. Consider a situation where a brand new teacher was hired midway through the school year and has no prior knowledge of how a Chromebook enhances learning experiences in a one to one setting. The tech coach must sit with their colleague and walk him through the various instances that a Chromebook would be used in a paperless learning environment. Coaches only enter this stance when they have been invited to provide an idea, or have asked permission to do so. They only stay in this stance long enough to give the teacher the information she needs to move forward again and then move back into another stance.

◆ *Collaborative Stance.* When it is clear that the teacher with whom you are working has some information or ideas, you may choose to take a collaborative stance. From the outside, this would look like two colleagues working together and contributing ideas as equal partners in the design of the solution. In a collaborative coaching stance, the coach helps frame or guide the conversation without directing it. For example, a teacher and a coach co-plan a literacy lesson that incorporates an online comic creator tool to make characters come to life. They might also problem-solve an implementation issue, or co-observe a teacher using a new strategy and then debrief together. When this stance is undertaken well, the coach has a chance to help model what a true professional collaboration can engender and both parties come away enriched from the interaction.

◆ *Facilitative Stance.* There are times when it is clear that the teacher already has ideas and solutions. Consider a forward-thinking social studies department that wants to not have students view virtual reality experiences, but actually create them on a program like CoSpaces EDU. The tech coach facilitates a planning process that will ultimately have students create virtual tours of the school district and community landmarks. In these situations, the job of the coach is to take on a facilitative stance and be a sounding board for the teacher as she works to think aloud and resolve her own problems. The teacher, not the coach, directs the flow of information, with the coach asking questions that help the teacher self-assess, refine thinking, and consider possibilities. For example, a facilitative coach might pose open-ended questions that clarify and deepen the teacher's thinking, facilitate a group of teachers as they consider a new initiative, or listen as a teacher analyzes student data and considers next steps.

Figure 2.3 Conversational Arc of Effective Mentoring/Coaching Conversations

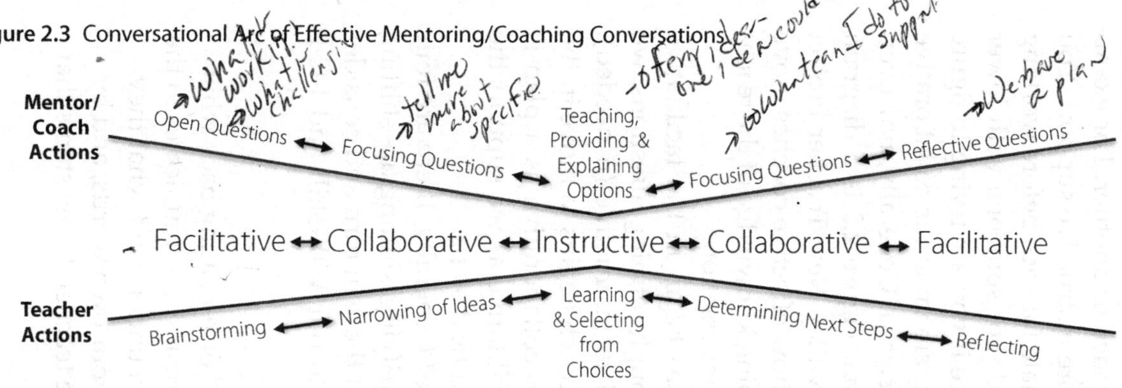

[handwritten annotations: "What skills...", "What will a mentor", "fellow templative?", "often, reflecting could be...", "important suggestion", "would be...", "mentorship?"]

Mentor/ Coach Actions

Open Questions — Focusing Questions — Teaching, Providing & Explaining Options — Focusing Questions — Reflective Questions

← Facilitative ↔ Collaborative ↔ Instructive ↔ Collaborative ↔ Facilitative →

Teacher Actions

Brainstorming — Narrowing of Ideas — Learning & Selecting from Choices — Determining Next Steps — Reflecting

Mentors/Coaches continually interpret visual and auditory cues to guide which stance to employ

Instructive	Collaborative	Facilitative
Flow of information is mainly from coach to teacher. The coach: • Directs interaction based on assessed needs • Provides information on teaching/procedures • Offers choices, suggestions with rationale	**Flow of information is relatively equal between coach and teacher. The coach:** • Guides interaction without controlling it • Co-constructs solutions/materials with teacher	**Flow of information is mainly from the teacher to the coach. The coach:** • Mainly listens while teacher shares • Acts as facilitator of teacher's thinking • Supports teacher in self-assessing
Before taking an Instructive stance, I might ask: • "Would you like me to offer some ideas?" • "Perhaps I can share some strategies that might be useful here?"	**Before taking a Collaborative stance, I might ask:** • "Should we look at this together?" • "What next steps might you and I take together?"	**Before taking a Facilitative stance, I might ask:** • "What is working right now in this situation?" • "What next steps are you considering?"
Instructive Coaching Moves: • Share process for analyzing student work • Model and instructional strategy • Offer menu of ways to differentiate instruction • Share thinking that leads to solution • Reference current research	**Collaborative Coaching Moves:** • Co-develop a lesson/unit • Co-plan a conversation with a parent/guardian • Problem solve issues of practice • Analyze examples of student work together • Co-observe another teacher and debrief	**Facilitative Coaching Moves:** • Facilitate group of teachers collaboratively planning • Listen as teacher analyzes student work • Post questions that clarify/deepen thinking

[handwritten at bottom] Entry point → something → in conversation that allow a person to stretch own.

(COPY) → Coaching Language

[handwritten top right: 3']

No one stance is more or less preferable. All are necessary at different times for all teachers. Our job as coaches is to stay curious, use our detective skills to monitor the conversation, and determine which stance is most beneficial for that teacher at that moment. Generally, there is a fluid continuum between and among the stances during the course of a coaching conversation. Depending on the teacher's level of will and skill around the topic you are discussing, you might linger longer in one stance or another. For example, someone who is lower skilled might need more instructive support. You might need to provide a set of options with rationale for each before working with the teacher to decide on a pathway forward. For someone with lower will, you might linger longer in a facilitative stance if you are trying to figure out what is creating the lack or will, or you might remain in the collaborative stance longer if they need motivation to move forward. Generally, however, we use all stances in the course of a conversation. Figure 2.3 is a diagram developed by Emily and the Santa Cruz/Silicon Valley New Teacher Project leadership team that might help you think about how effective coaches move between these stances depending on their developing knowledge of the teacher's strengths and needs and the purpose of the conversation.

As you can see, many coaching conversations begin in the facilitative realm with big open-ended questions. Then, through refining questions, we often move into collaborative conversation, and to instructive (if needed). Then, as the plan to move forward emerges, the coach begins to move in the other direction on the continuum; first back into collaborative as a plan is developed and refined and, finally, back into facilitative as we support the teacher in reflecting on the journey, learnings, and next steps.

So, what do these different stances sound like? Generally, there are four categories of coaching language: paraphrasing, clarifying, shifting up–shifting down, and offering suggestions. Let's take each of these in turn and consider how these types of coaching language connect to our Will-Skill and I-C-F Frameworks in the world of the tech coach:

1. *Paraphrasing.* This is not "parrot-phrasing" or repeating back what someone has said word for word. Paraphrasing communicates to the teacher that you are listening carefully and understand what they are saying by restating what you hear in your own words, and by summarizing and organizing ideas for the teacher. Some stems that might be useful are things like:

   ◆ "So, what I am hearing you say . . ."
   ◆ "It sounds like . . ."
   ◆ "I'm hearing several important ideas . . ."
   ◆ "I want to check that I am understanding, I hear . . ."

A tech coach might say, "So, it sounds like you are looking for a way to better communicate with parents about student progress that doesn't require a lot of additional hours on your part. Is that correct? Would a tool like Google Classroom fit your needs?"

As we discussed in Chapter 1, active listening is a critical coaching action. Taking the time to check what you are hearing is a critical first step to showing the teacher you care about them and want to help. It also helps you work as a detective to figure out their will and skill levels, i.e. what the teacher already knows or doesn't know, what they care about, and how they are thinking about the topic. Understanding this can help you to determine what stance they need you to take (I-C-F) to best meet their needs.

2. *Clarifying.* As you listen, there may be some things you do not fully understand, have questions about, or want to explore further with the teacher. Sometimes, in education, we struggle to communicate with one another because we use a lot of jargon, use different words to mean the same thing, or use the same words to mean different things! Clarifying builds on paraphrasing by allowing you to further check your understanding of ideas, words, concepts, or feelings you may be unclear about coming from the speaker. Frames for clarifying questions might sound like:

   ◆ "Say more about . . ."
   ◆ " Can you tell me more about . . ."
   ◆ "When you say___, what do you mean?"
   ◆ "Can you give me an example of . . .?"
   ◆ "What connections do you see between ___ and ____?"

   For example, a coach might ask, "Can you give me an example of how you are currently using technology to communicate with parents versus what you want to have happen? Are you using social media or a blogging service to disseminate information?" These questions are not meant to be a chance for you to satisfy your own personal curiosity about something a teacher has said. Rather, they are a chance to dig deeper into the conversation, and hone in further on where the teacher is with her will/skill today and what she needs from you in the conversation. Continue paraphrasing and asking clarifying questions until you get a clearer sense from the teacher about what, specifically, the teacher knows and needs before moving forward.

3. *Shifting Up–Shifting Down.* Sometimes as you listen to a colleague, it becomes clear that they are stuck down in the weeds of the

work—in the details, in specific examples, in the minutiae of the discussion so much so that they cannot see beyond what has happened to other possibilities. In these cases, your role as a coach is to support the teacher in shifting up—moving from the details to the bigger picture. Laura Lipton and Bruce Wellman (*Mentoring Matters*, 2001) suggest that coaches can help teachers shift up to reconnect with their values, goals, intentions, beliefs, purposes, and assumptions. Doing so helps them come unstuck from the details and begin to think about bigger possibilities again. To help folks shift up, coaches might use word like:

◆ "So, a goal for us might be . . ."
◆ "Remind me again about the purpose you have for . . ."
◆ "What is your broader intention for . . .:

An example might sound like, "I hear your goal is to better connect with parents about student progress. How is the current process you are using helping you to achieve that goal? What might be missing? Does your goal take into consideration the fact that all parents are on their smartphones now and want information with a tap of the screen?"

On the other hand, sometimes as you listen to a colleague, you find they are only talking at a very high level—the level of ideals, abstractions, theories, or broad concepts—in a way that is preventing them from making forward progress. In these cases, the coachee may need some support shifting down from abstractions and concepts into more concrete examples/non-examples, strategies, options, decisions, actions, or details in order to move forward (Lipton & Wellman, 2001). As a coach, you can support this shifting down with phrases such as:

◆ "So, we want to establish a procedure for . . ."
◆ "What might a strategy be that would help you . . ."
◆ "What would an example of that look like in practice?"

An example might sound something like, "If your goal is to connect with parents more easily using technology, what decisions do we need to make that will help you begin to achieve that goal?"

The questions and stems you see listed and in Figure 2.3 may support you in thinking about what this coaching language might sound like as you move across the continuum. Again, the goal is to help your colleague raise or maintain their level of will and skill by finding success with implementation and developing and articulating with your support a process for making decisions that they can replicate independently.

"We Need to Talk": How to Have Difficult Conversations That Build Trust

In most situations, the kind of tailored support structure described in this chapter will help coachees move forward in their ability and confidence to effectively implement technology. However, there are situations in which progress does not occur over a period of time and it becomes clear that a deeper issue needs to be addressed before progress can be made again. Many coaches shy away from having tough conversations with coachees because they are afraid that the coachee will get mad and stop trusting the coach. While this is a real concern, the alternative—not having a conversation and continuing to see no improvement—can also lead to loss of trust. If the coachee doesn't see growth in his/her practice as a result of meeting with you, how long do you think they will continue to trust that you can help them? Having tough conversations early can actually help to get a team to grow closer and get unstuck so that work can continue and trust can grow. It's critical that you don't let situations fester for too long. The question becomes, then, what do you say and how do you say it so trust grows and you are able to begin making progress together again?

1. *Deciding When to Have the Talk.* Timing is critical to the success of hard conversations. You need to make sure you have enough time and space to talk about the issue fully. It's not a great idea, therefore, to broach a difficult subject when you only have five minutes left in your meeting or while passing each other in the hall. Make an appointment to meet with the person before or after school or at some other time when you both can pay full attention to the topic of your conversation. As a note of caution, when you set the appointment, the coachee may ask, "What's this about?" Avoid the initial desire to launch into the issue right then and there. Let them know you have something you want to talk about with them, but that this isn't the best place to talk about it. Let them know you look forward to talking to them soon. Then, walk away.

   Location is also important. Hard conversations are hard enough without having an audience, so make sure you have a private place to talk. Avoid classrooms where students or other teachers might walk in, the staffroom, or other public spaces. Consider an office with a door you can close if one is available to you.

2. *What Do I Say?* Take some time to plan out what you want to say before you go into the meeting. You need to make sure that you are ready to talk about the issue in a calm and coherent way without emotion coloring your words and that you are ready to really listen and problem solve with the coachee so that the situation resolves itself successfully.

Like all good coaching, you also have to be ready to approach the conversation with the positive presupposition that the coachee wants to improve and that, together, you can come to a positive resolution for the issue. You also need to come ready with a sense of curiosity to understand what is happening and why from the coachees' point of view so that you can seek to resolve the situation in a way that is going to be best for this coachee. All of this takes planning and prep on your part.

Generally, there are five parts to a good, hard conversation:

1. State your common goal. Begin by reminding the coachee that you are here to support them and that you have a common goal of success for both the coachee and his/her students. This might sound something like, "I am so glad you and I have the opportunity to work together this year. I know we both want your students to have success with Google Classroom and I know that, together, we can make that happen."

2. State the issue with evidence to back it up. Clearly, but succinctly, define the challenge you are seeing right now and why you think this is an issue. Make sure to use non-evaluative statements and use specific evidence to back it up. This might sound something like, "Out of our last five scheduled meetings, you have cancelled two of them at the last minute and missed one without letting me know. It is difficult for us to make forward progress when we do not meet regularly. It is also challenging for my schedule when you cancel meetings at the last minute or miss meetings without letting me know."

3. Listen to what the other person has to say. After you state the issue, invite the coachee to share what they are thinking and feeling about the issue you have raised. Be sure to remind them that you are there to support them and believe you can resolve the situation successfully. This might sound something like, "I know that we can work together to resolve this issue because we want the same thing. So, I want to hear what you are thinking and feeling about this issue I have raised. What should I know about the situation that I might not?"

   While you listen to your coachee share, use your active listening skills to truly hear what the other person is saying. Work hard to turn off the voice in your head that is formulating what you want to say next and, instead, seek to understand their perspective. Use your coaching language (i.e. paraphrasing, clarifying) to make sure you understand.

4. Collaborate to develop solutions. Once the coachee has shared and you feel you have developed an understanding of the situation from their perspective, the next stage is to brainstorm some strategies to move forward. As you have been listening to the coachee, you were hopefully using your coaching detective skills to seek entry points that you might be able to use as a starting point for this brainstorming. As you invite the coachee to share ideas and as you share ideas, connecting back to things the coachee said is a great place to start. It builds trust because it shows you were listening and trying to adapt to meet their needs while, at the same time, holding the coachee accountable to make the situation better. This might sound like, "I am so glad to hear that you also are frustrated with our inability to meet and the impact this is having on your Google Classroom implementation. Thank you for sharing some of the challenges you are having with scheduling. I hear that Thursday afternoons have become problematic for us to meet. I am wondering if you have some ideas about what we can do to resolve this situation. For example, is there another time during the week that it would be better for us to meet?" and, "I also want to make sure we have a plan in place should we need to change our meeting again in the future. What agreements can we make about when and how we might reschedule a meeting?"

Work with the coachee to agree upon solutions. To support buy- in, ask the coachee to restate the agreement in his/her own words instead of you voicing the agreement. You could say something like, "So, it sounds like we have a plan for how we can move forward here. Can you say what you understand about our agreement? I want to make sure we are on the same page."

5. Make a plan to make the solution a success. Once you have an agreement in place, make a plan to implement it successfully. Also make a plan to check in after a certain period of time about this agreement to make sure it is moving forward smoothly. A common mistake coaches make is that they have the hard conversation and then they think they never have to bring it up again. Revisiting these agreements after a set period of time ensures accountability for both the coach and the coachee to continue to make the situation better. It builds trust because it is clear that you follow through on what you say you will do and that, as a result, things are improving. You might say something like, "Thank you so much for talking with me about this today. I am encouraged that our new plan to move our meetings to

Wednesdays before school and having me email you a day in advance to confirm our meeting will improve our ability to meet. I would love for us to check in about how this is working in a month just to make sure this new plan is helping. Can we add this topic to our meeting agenda on March 12th?"

Below is a graphic organizer that can help you plan out hard conversations with your coachees (and others) with the method described above (Figure 2.4).

3. *Okay, I Had the Talk . . . Now What?* Congratulations! You had "the talk" with your coachee and it went well. Great job. In the vast majority of situations, having the conversation and following up on that conversation as you laid out in your plan are enough to overcome the issue at hand. If a new issue comes up, you now have the skills to have these types of conversations. You have also created an understanding with your coachee about how you will handle a

Figure 2.4 Planning for Hard Coaching Conversations

---

1. What is your common goal with your coachee?

- What do you both want?
- What role does technology play in your goal setting?

2. State the issue with evidence to back it up

- What is your concern? Why is it concerning to you? How is it connected to your common goal?
- What evidence do you have that this is an issue?
- How is technology enhancing or obstructing what you are trying to accomplish?

3. Listen to what the other person has to say

- What is their perspective on the issue?
- What entry points are they offering that might help you both to come to a resolution?

4. Collaborate to develop solutions

- What would a good solution look like for you?
  - What is non-negotiable for you as a coach (consider how you balance teacher needs, your needs/schedule, and your common goal)?
  - What could you adjust that would still allow you to strike this balance?
- What resources might be needed to enact this solution (consider materials, people, learning, etc.)?
- How will technology support learning and teaching?

5. Make a plan to make the solution a success

- When and how will you check in?
  - What will happen if you are not making progress?
  - Who else would need to be involved if progress is not being made?
  - How will the effective implementation of technology be assessed as you look to meet the learning outcomes for students?

---

lack of progress. If another issue arises, or the same issue persists, you can return to this process again and address the situation again.

Having hard conversations that help you and your coachee begin making progress again in a timely manner is an important skill in your coaching tool kit. While it can feel scary to engage in these types of conversations for a variety of reasons, failing to do so can lead to a lot more issues in the long run.

Putting It All Together

In this chapter, we have explored how to work from a stance of curiosity as a coach, determine a coachee's level of will and skill with technology, and how to adapt coaching stances and language to create a coaching scenario that is just right for a colleagues' level of readiness. We have also discussed what to do when coaching isn't working and we need to have a talk to get unstuck and move forward again. This coaching skill set is critical to the success of any one-on-one tech coaching endeavor. When we pay attention to the needs of the adults in front of us, seek to work with them instead of on them, and adapt our methods to best suit their needs, everyone comes out a winner.

In the next chapter, we will explore how tech coaches can success-fully take the skills we've unpacked in this chapter and apply them to coaching teachers individually around technology.

References

Glickman, C. (2002). *Leadership for Learning: How to Help Teachers Succeed.* Alexandria, VA: ASCD.

Jackson, R. (2013). *Never Underestimate Your Teachers.* Alexandria, VA: ASCD.

Landsberg, M. (1996). *Tao of Coaching: Boost Your Effectiveness at Work by Inspiring and Developing Those Around You.* London: Profile Books, Ltd.

Lipton, L. & Wellman, B.M. (2001). *Mentoring Matters: A Practical Guide to Learning-Focused Relationships.* Charlotte, NC: MiraVia LLC.

3

Coaching for Meaningful Technology Integration

Technology is a vehicle for 21st century learning. Having a strong pedagogy has to come before technology. Otherwise, it is just bells and whistles. It might engage our students, but it is not adding to the bigger purpose of teaching and learning. Being able to envision how to leverage technology to design future ready learning experiences for students comes more readily for teachers who have an understanding of best practices.

Chanmi Chun, Mentor/Instructional Coach

[Teachers] need to know how technology can support collaboration and communication and how it can help to form learning communities. I don't take a "technology first" approach when planning lessons for my students. I don't squeeze blogging artificially into some lesson just to have my students blog. This is like having a hammer and treating every lesson like a nail. I start with my instructional objectives and choose instructional strategies based on these objectives. At times, this might mean utilizing no technology at all for a lesson. Other times, it might involve developing a fully online lesson where students communicate via a chat room. The important component, however, is that we as educators need to have a variety of pedagogical strategies to draw upon when we plan and teach lessons. We wouldn't want to artificially squeeze blogging into a lesson any more than we would want to lecture to students every day. We absolutely need to focus on what the pedagogy requires. But we also need to have a strong understanding of what technology can offer in order to make informed pedagogical decisions.

Oliver Dreon, Ph.D., Associate Professor, Millersville University

If you haven't guessed by now, we are fans of educational technology and believe in its power to enhance learning experiences for students. However, we are also quite clear that technology is no more than an instructional tool. It is not something we encourage schools, teachers, or coaches to employ in classrooms merely for the sake of using technology. We strongly believe that pedagogically effective teaching, coupled with some technology infused student activities, can help to promote the engagement and empowerment for students. We want to underline what we just wrote in the last sentence— pedagogical decisions must come first and decisions about appropriate technology applications second. However, this is not always what happens when technology gets involved.

Educators often fall prey to activity-driven planning processes. Instead of planning with the end in mind and then working backward to determine how students will show us what they know and what sequence of instructional experiences they will need to have in order to move from where they are now to this goal, teachers find an activity they love and try to plan around that. While these activities might be engaging, the learning that occurs is generally disconnected from outcomes that don't help students make progress. We see many instances where teachers use technology in the same way. They see a technology or an application that they like and try to plan around that instead of using the technology as a tool to support learning.

Eric Sheninger writes artfully about this topic in a 2016 *EdTech Magazine* article:

> When implem   successfully sustaining a mobile learning initiative   llow the device to drive instruction.   ts should never be bui   education should be bu   to improve student ou   e initiative should be t
>
> When it   t the feeling that the lea   st for the sake of "using   me that could be dedica   es into a huge waste of
>
> Most   ver, we cannot assume   ort their learning. Thi   ign is necessary, first and foremo   nd better assessments firmly in place, the stage   to truly begin to own their learning in ways never imagined. The key is to determine

what we want our students to know, and then let them have a choice as to how they will demonstrate or apply their learning. This not only adds relevance and meaning to the learning but also takes the pressure off the educators from having to learn how to use an endless number of tools.

Our primary job in coaching educators at all levels around the use of technology, therefore, is helping them to understand how they can leverage technology as a useful tool for getting at their outcomes, and not just as an engagement strategy that is used for its own sake.

In this chapter, we will explore:

◆ frameworks for technology integration;
◆ lesson planning with tech in mind;
◆ technology for 21st-century learning, social-emotional learning, and educational equity; and
◆ engaging families with technology.

Frameworks for Technology Integration

All teachers who wish to become potential edtech coaches should learn information regarding both the SAMR and TPACK method of technology integration. SAMR is most often used when teaching about technology tools, such as Google Classroom. TPACK is often used after conducting a needs analysis of a school district or organization and implementing a technology plan/proposal.

Krista Welz, School Librarian and College Professor

A useful starting point for most tech coaches is to have a framework, or series of frameworks, which define how they understand best practices in edtech integration. In this chapter, we offer three such models that we feel can be strong starting points: TPACK, SAMR, and Technology Use by Quadrant within the Rigor Relevance Framework.

1. The TPACK Model

Most educators think about two domains of knowledge they must possess—content knowledge (the subject matter that they teach) and pedagogical knowledge (knowledge about how to teach). In 1986, Lee Shulman countered this bifurcation of knowledge, writing that effective teachers work in the overlap between these two knowledge sets. Coining the phrase, pedagogical content knowledge (PCK), Shulman contends that effective teachers have a set of knowledge about how to effectively teach their subject matter. Twenty years later, Koehler and Mishra saw the addition of technology to the classroom as something not connected to content, pedagogy, or PCK, but rather as a third body of knowledge to which teachers need to attend. They developed a new framework called TPACK (Technological Pedagogical Content Knowledge) which looks at how the three domains shown in the graphic below (Figure 3.1) work together to make the content more accessible and engaging for students:

Figure 3.1 The TPACK Model

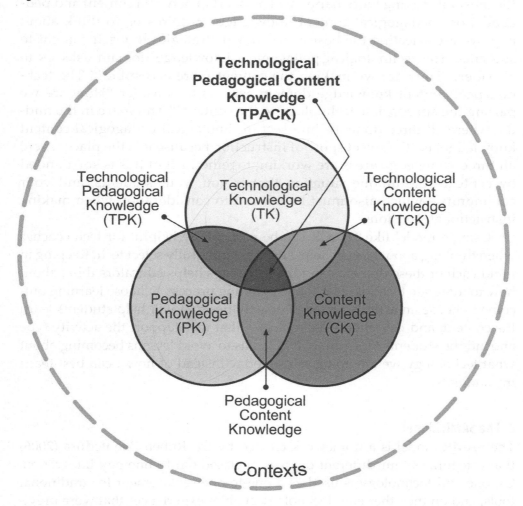

The content knowledge is the "what" we teach—the subject matter of the lesson (i.e. math, science, art history). The pedagogical knowledge is the "how" we teach—the instructional tools teachers use to make the content more accessible to students (i.e. direct instruction, inquiry, modeling, small group discussion). The technological knowledge is selecting an appropriate partner tool. This body of knowledge allows us to consider what tool we could use that would allow us to make the content more accessible to students while supporting the pedagogical strategy we have identified that will best help to deliver this information to students (i.e. movie, virtual manipulatives, SMARTboard).

The overlaps between these three larger domains are the place where the most interesting work happens. The overlap between content and pedagogy, or "pedagogical content knowledge" requires us to think about how we are selecting the best instructional strategies to teach content to students. The technological pedagogical knowledge domain asks us to consider, "How are we making the content more accessible?" The technological content knowledge domain asks us to consider "How are we pairing the appropriate technology to the content?" The space in the middle where all three domains intersect (technological pedagogical content knowledge) is "the sweet spot" of instruction because it is the place where all three knowledge areas are working together. All of this is surrounded by context—the unique situation that is you, your students, and your community—which also must be taken into consideration when making instructional decisions.

Using a model like TPACK can be particularly helpful for tech coaches when thinking about how to help clients meaningfully select tech. Keeping in mind each of these domains and their overlaps helps educators think about how to integrate technology into the planning process—choose learning outcomes, choose an activity or series of activities that will help students learn the content, and *then* choose technologies that will support the activity type and aid the students in learning. It helps us to avoid lessons becoming about what technology we are going to use today instead of how I can best teach my students.

2. The SAMR Model

The SAMR model is a framework created by Dr. Ruben Puentedura (2006) that categorizes four different degrees of classroom technology integration. On one end technology is used as a one-to-one replacement for traditional tools, and on the other end, technology enables experiences that were previously impossible without it. The model provides teachers with clear direction

Figure 3.2 The SAMR Model

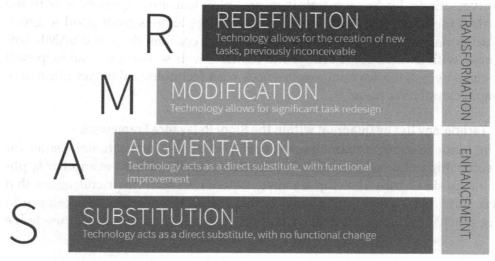

www.hippasus.com/rrpweblog/

on how technology can enhance and transform learning experiences at various levels of implementation. Take a look at Figure 3.2 for more information about the stages of the model:

During Brad's time as a school and district leader, he observed educational environments that touch on all four types of technology integration. Additionally, Brad, working alongside his tremendous technology coaches, has witnessed lesson and unit plans pop in ways once thought unimaginable. Here are four examples of what SAMR might look like in an environment where technology coaches support their colleagues with relevant technology integration . . .

- ◆ **Substitution:** A student uses a Google Doc to take notes digitally in place of pen and paper.
- ◆ **Augmentation:** A student shares his Google Doc that contains a writing assignment with his teacher who can then provide timely feedback using the comment feature.
- ◆ **Modification:** Students in social studies class have the option of creating a website with Google Sites to show what they know about a certain part of the Civil War.
- ◆ **Redefinition:** A teacher, with the support of the technology coach, plans a virtual reality tour using Google Expeditions to enhance students' knowledge of the assassination of Abraham Lincoln at Ford's Theatre.

As an instructional coach using technology, it's important to conduct conversations, lead group trainings, and plan learning experiences with the SAMR model in mind as a framework to move lessons from good to great. Additionally, it's important that instructional coaches share the SAMR language with leaders at the school and district levels so that they can help staff focus on engaging learning experiences with technology that can ultimately impact student success.

3. Technology Use by Quadrant within the Rigor Relevance Framework

The Rigor Relevance Framework, developed by the International Center for Leadership in Education (ICLE) gives instructional coaches yet another applicable guide to truly develop learning experiences with their colleagues that will have students thinking and creating at high levels. As you can see in Figure 3.3, the more students are exposed to various forms of knowledge

Figure 3.3 Rigor/Relevance Framework

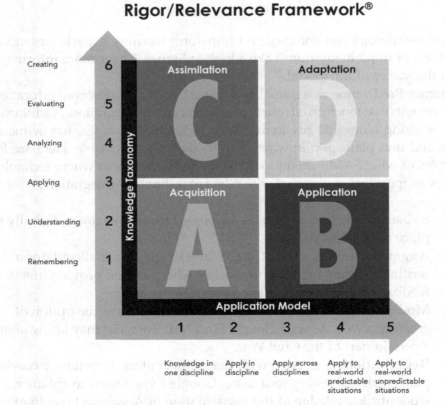

Figure 3.4 Technology Use by Quadrant

Technology Use By Quadrant

KNOWLEDGE TAXONOMY

6 CREATING
CAN THE STUDENT CREATE NEW PRODUCTS OR POINTS OF VIEW?

5 EVALUATING
CAN THE STUDENT JUSTIFY A STAND OR DECISION?

4 ANALYZING
CAN THE STUDENT DISTINGUISH BETWEEN THE DIFFERENT PARTS?

3 APPLYING
CAN THE STUDENT USE THE INFORMATION IN A NEW WAY?

2 UNDERSTANDING
CAN THE STUDENT EXPLAIN IDEAS OR CONCEPTS?

1 REMEMBERING
CAN THE STUDENT RECALL OR REMEMBER THE INFORMATION?

Quadrant C

VERBS
- Analyze
- Classify
- Diagram
- Evaluate
- Examine
- Explain
- Infer
- Judge
- Research
- Summarize

EXAMPLES
- Hyperlinking
- Media Clipping/Cropping
- Monitoring
- Photos/Video
- Programming
- Reverse Engineering
- Software Cracking
- Testing
- Validating Resources
- Video Editing

Quadrant D

VERBS
- Argue
- Conclude
- Create
- Explore
- Invent
- Modify
- Plan
- Predict
- Rate

EXAMPLES
- Animating
- Audio Casting
- Blog Commenting
- Broadcasting
- Collaborating
- Composing—GarageBand
- Digital Storytelling
- Directing
- Mashing-Mixing/Remixing
- Modifying/Game Modding
- Networking
- Photo/Video Blogging
- Podcasting
- Reviewing

Quadrant A

VERBS
- Define
- Identify
- Label
- List
- Locate
- Memorize
- Name
- Recite
- Record
- Select

EXAMPLES
- Bullets & Lists
- Creating & Naming Folders
- Editing
- Highlighting/Selecting
- Internet Searching
- Loading
- Typing
- Using a Mouse
- Word Doc

Quadrant B

VERBS
- Apply
- Construct
- Demonstrate
- Dramatize
- Illustrate
- Interpret
- Interview
- Sequence
- Solve

EXAMPLES
- Advanced Searching
- Annotating
- Blogs
- Google Docs
- Hacking
- Operating/Running a Program
- Posting—Social Media
- Replying—Commenting
- Sharing
- Social Bookmarking
- Subscribing to RSS feed
- Tagging
- Texting
- Uploading
- Web Authoring

APPLICATION MODEL

1	2	3	4	5
KNOWLEDGE IN ONE DISCIPLINE	APPLICATION WITHIN ONE DISCIPLINE	APPLICATION ACROSS DISCIPLINES	APPLICATION TO REAL-WORLD PREDICTABLE SITUATIONS	APPLICATION TO REAL-WORLD UNPREDICTABLE SITUATIONS

and the more engaging the applications, the better. The Technology Use by Quadrant diagram, Figure 3.4, blends technology within the Framework to give teachers and students viable options to show what they understand about the topic at hand.

Lesson Planning With Tech in Mind

Models like TPACK, SAMR, and the Technology Use by Quadrant in the Rigor/Relevance Framework are helpful for teachers and coaches to consider at a theoretical level. However, sometimes it is difficult to turn those concepts into reality. We have developed a lesson planning template that tech coaches may find useful to use as a whole, adapt, or select pieces from to use in conversations with educators. Using a plan like this as the basis for a coaching conversation can help both you and the educator you are supporting to ensure you are both clear about the lesson objectives, the content, and the sound pedagogical decisions that need to be made first before an appropriate technological tool can be selected to support and enhance the instructional decisions. As you review the lesson planning tool below (Figure 3.5), think about each box as an entry point. If you recall from Chapter 1, an entry point is a natural place where a teacher helps you learn something about what he really needs and allows you to enter the conversation in a way that is most helpful for that teacher. What entry points could a tool like this create for you in coaching conversations?

You may have noticed that each section in this tool contains questions that a coach could ask a teacher to help understand or develop a lesson plan based on the TPACK, SAMR, and/or the Rigor/Relevance Framework models. There are a number of entry points upon which a coach might capitalize depending on how the teacher approaches the subject. For example, if a teacher comes to you asking for support using Newsela in her classroom, you can begin the conversation in the "Technological Supports" section to better understand what she thinks the value of this particular tool might be. Then, you can move to the "Standards and Learning Objectives" section to better understand her content and skill goals. Then, you can move to the "Pedagogical Sequence" section to understand how she is trying to teach this content. Only then will you have enough information to understand if, when, and how this particular application would best support her. On the other hand, if a teacher approaches you asking for ideas around making his math lesson more accessible for his English learners, you can enter this tool at the "Planning with Students in Mind"

Figure 3.5 Backwards Design for the Digital Age

The purpose of this tool is to support the development of well-structured lessons based on the TPACK model as well as an understanding of students' strengths and needs.

Standards and Learning Objectives	
Standard(s) or standard component(s) to be addressed in this lesson, lesson sequence, or unit What is essential for students to learn? What are the objective(s) and/or essential question(s)? *(What do you want students to understand, know, and do by the end of this instructional sequence?)*	
Planning with Students in Mind	
What are students' strengths with this content/skill? *(What do they already understand/know? What can they already do?)*	
What are students' challenges with this content/skill? *(What gaps might they have in their understanding/knowledge? What can they not yet do?)*	
What modifications will you need to keep in mind for special populations of students? *(Students with special needs, gifted students, English learners, etc.)*	
Assessment for Learning	
How will you summatively assess students' ability to meet your objectives?	
What set of formative assessments will help you know students are making progress towards your objectives during instruction?	
Pedagogical Sequence	
What sequence of pedagogical moves will you need to make in order to scaffold students from where they are to your outcomes? *(Consider using a model such as gradual release, inquiry, or backwards design to plan this sequence)*	
How might your pedagogical sequence include 21st- century learning skills? *(Communication, collaboration, critical thinking, creativity).* What would you need to teach or reinforce in order to help foster these skills?	
What might you need to plan to ensure the environment is conducive to learning? • What whole class/small group/individual work procedures might need to be taught? *(Consider technology as well as collaborative routines).* How might you teach or reinforce these? • What social-emotional learning (SEL) competencies might need to be encouraged? *(Self-awareness, self-management, responsible decision-making, relationship skills, social awareness).* How might you teach or reinforce these?	
Technological Supports	

• How might instructional technology:
  ○ Make content more accessible to some/all students? *(Technological content knowledge)*
  ○ Enhance your pedagogical choices including 21st-century and SEL skill development? *(Technological pedagogical knowledge)*
  ○ Support students in showing you what they know/can do? *(Assessment)*
• What technologies might you use to achieve these goals? *(Use SAMR model — Augmentation, Modification, and Redefinition — to consider how tech can enhance instruction and learning)*
• How will all students access these tools equitably?
• What instruction would students need to effectively use these tools?	

Reflection	
After delivering this lesson sequence, reflect on what went well. *(Consider content, pedagogy, and technology)* • Why were these pieces successful? • What will you do next as a result of these successes?	
What was less successful in this lesson sequence? *(Consider content, pedagogy, and technology)* • Why were these pieces less successful? • What did you need to adjust and why? • What will you do next as a result of these experiences?	

section to better understand who his students are and what they need. Then, you can move us to the "Standards and Learning Objectives" section to understand what he is trying to teach, then down to the "Pedagogical Sequence" section before finally helping him to thoughtfully select a tool to help him meet his students where they are and support them in moving towards his objectives. If you are entering a conversation with a teacher and don't yet know where the conversation is going technology-wise, you might want to follow the advice of Millersville University's Learning Technologies Librarian and Director of the Digital Learning Studio, Greg Szczyrbak (personal interview):

> I always start by asking, "What are you working on? I think this is a better question than how can I help you. When you go to Home Depot they don't ask you what tool do you need; they ask you what are you working on? From there they help you figure out what to get. They don't know all the things I know or can do for them, so they can't answer the question about how I can help them.

This simple change of stance helps keep coaching from being transactional and moves it into the collaborative realm. You have a chance to figure out together.

Depending on the teacher's level of confidence and knowledge (will and skill) with technology, they may be ready to move beyond using tools that are substitutes for paper and pencil tasks (low on the SAMR scale) to consider using technological tools that would allow them to modify or even redefine the way they are instructing using technology (higher on the SAMR scale). A savvy tech coach will have a number of options ready to offer the teacher depending on their readiness levels in each of the scenarios above.

We want to be clear that not every teacher or every coaching conversation will require you to use this tool in its entirety. It is perfectly fine to select pieces to discuss and leave others out. We also know that, for some teachers, sharing this tool with them might be a helpful move. However, we also know that in other coaching situations you may wish to use this tool only as a resource for yourself—meaning you keep it on your clipboard to support your coaching discussion and/or to take notes for yourself, but do not place it in front of the teacher. Use your coaching detective skills, your skill/will diagnosis skills, and your coaching language (see Chapter 1 for more on these topics) to make this determination on a case-by-case basis.

Figure 3.6 Small Learning Communities with the Station Rotation Model

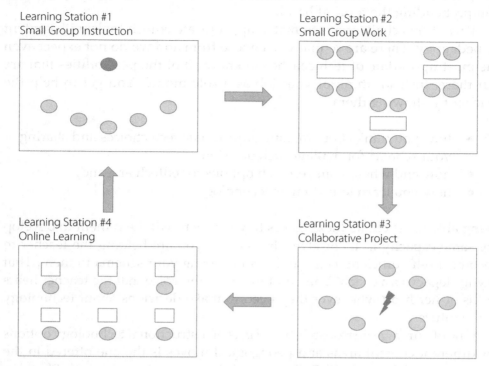

Reprinted from Catlin Tucker et al's., *Blended Learning in Action* by permission from Corwin

Let's look at an example of a lesson plan using the template above. An elementary teacher you are coaching regularly uses stations as part of her math instruction. She has seen others use technology as part of stations, but never very effectively. After learning more about her lesson objectives, the needs and strengths of her students around working in groups, and her pedagogical plans for station work, you provide her with information related to the Station Rotation Model (Figure 3.6) developed by Catlin Tucker.

The teacher likes this idea and asks you to help her integrate technology into a few of these stations. After learning more about her content and student collaboration goals for each station, you agree that at one station students could use a program like Educreations (www.educreations.com/) to show others how to solve certain types of math problems. In another station, students will use a website like Desmos (https://teacher.desmos. com/) to dig deep into variety of digitized math problems. These are just two of many options you could suggest. The sky's the limit! The bottom line here is that it's really important to blend activities that reside in both the physical and virtual worlds so that students have multiple options for comprehending the topic at hand.

Part of this challenge is to match appropriate edtech tools with content or pedagogy. There are so many to choose from and we do not expect even the most up-to-date of tech coaches to know all of the possibilities that are out there. Instead, think of your job as a role model. You get to help the teacher by showing them

- ◆ how you think about making appropriate tech choices and sharing your schema for making such decisions;
- ◆ how and where your research options for edtech are, and;
- ◆ how you learn to use a new technology.

Being able to articulate these pieces to your client will help them to develop the same capacity in themselves. In essence, you are helping the teacher to become a self-sufficient tech user by transferring your schema to them. That is your legacy as a coach! You will forever be the voice that the teacher hears in his or her head whenever they need to make decisions about technology in the future.

One of our favorite research-based lists of instructional technology options for different content areas and pedagogical moves is the one offered in the 2010 article "'Grounded' Technology Integration: Instructional Planning Using Curriculum-Based Activity Type Taxonomies" by Harris and Hoffer et al. While there have been thousands of new technologies developed since this list came out, the schema the researchers use to match tech with content and skills may help you and your client to brainstorm other similar and more modern edtech tools.

Helping your client to understand a schema for appropriately selecting and integrating technology into their planning and instruction is a tremendously valuable way coaches can improve teaching and learning outcomes in their setting. We hope that the TPACK, SAMR, and Rigor/Relevance Framework schemas coupled with the Backwards Design for the Digital Age tool will help you to feel ready to enter and structure coaching conversations with teachers in ways that grow their confidence, their knowledge, and their practice.

Technology for Social-Emotional Learning, 21st-Century Learning, and Educational Equity

You might have noticed that the Backwards Design for the Digital Age tool we offered above included questions related to Social-Emotional Learning

(SEL), 21st- Century Learning, and educational equity. We believe that one of the most important, and often overlooked, conversations educators need to have around technology is about these topics. Let's take each one in turn and consider the intersections between technology and these important topics.

1. *Social-Emotional Learning (SEL)*: Sometimes referred to as "soft skills" or "non-cognitive skills," SEL competencies are the skills that help us to manage our feelings, create positive relationships, and engage with others in a positive manner. The Collaborative for Academic, Social, and Emotional Learning (CASEL), has identified five core components of SEL that are necessary for success in all aspects of life: self-awareness, self-management, responsible decision-making, relationship skills, social awareness. SEL-proficient individuals tend to have higher levels of mental well-being, greater success in higher education and the workplace, and higher income levels than their less proficient peers (Oberle, Domitrovich, Meyers, & Weissberg, 2016) The current trend towards more rigorous standards such as Common Core, Next Generation Science Standards, and the C3 Social Science Standards all require students to take more risks, engage with challenging tasks for longer periods of time, and collaborate more with others than ever before. Researchers have begun to note that students who have stronger SEL skills are more successful with these new standards, regardless of other other variables, than those who do not have these skills.

   While these are skills that should be taught in person and embedded throughout the day, there is plenty of room for technology to play a part in strengthening students' SEL skills as well. Here are a few examples:

   a. Self-Directed Learning. Students are generally more engaged and learn better when they are learning what they want to learn, at their own pace, and in their own style. Teachers can think about how technology can create more options for students to take ownership of their learning, set goals, make choices about how they access information, and keep track of their progress. This supports the development of SEL skills like self-management and responsible decision-making.

   b. Personalization. Working in a student's zone of proximal development (ZPD)—that place where learning is neither too easy nor too hard—helps students keep from being bored by too easy content or frustrated by content that is too hard. Edtech that uses adaptive processes to tailor the level of learning to each student as she progresses can help students access the appropriate level of challenge more effectively than any human could for a classroom of students. Working continuously in one's ZPD also supports students' confidence and self-manages skill growth.

c. Building Agency. Technology, specifically games, is a powerful tool for engaging, motivating, and helping students in learning how to problem-solve, make decisions, and empathize. Success with the game builds confidence in themselves.

d. Collaboration. Technology allows students to work together in a wide range of ways from developing a common document to interacting in a game together. Through this kind of interaction, students can develop positive relationship skills and social awareness as well as practice the self-awareness and self-management skills necessary for successful interactions with others.

As coaches work with teachers to select and implement edtech choices, they need to have an awareness of how these tools can benefit the development of SEL skills or consider what SEL skills students will need to practice employing during the use of the technology. Asking questions during planning about students' areas of SEL strength or need can help both you and the teacher plan for successful instruction.

2. *21st-Century Learning*: Sometimes called the 4Cs of learning, 21st-century learning focuses on the skill set necessary for success in the modern world. Technology provides a wonderful opportunity to enhance instruction and practice of these domains. Take a look at the 4Cs below and consider how technology could support teachers and students in teaching, practicing, and building each of these domains:

a. Communication: sharing thoughts, ideas, questions, and solutions with one another.

b. Collaboration: working together to reach a goal—putting talent, expertise, and smarts to work.

c. Critical Thinking: looking at problems in a new way, linking learning across subjects and disciplines.

d. Creativity: trying new approaches to get things done equals innovation and invention.

Chanmi Chun, a mentor and instructional coach in San Jose, California, described in a personal interview the role of the coach in helping teachers develop 21st-century skills using technology:

Coaching is about understanding what those 21st-century shifts in thinking are and then helping teachers think about how can you use technology to support the students to do those things—be communicators, use it to give each other feedback, and collaborate. Technology provides a way to make connections with others. If you can learn from someone in a different country—having a face you've seen, having actually talked to that person—maybe what you'd thought of that culture has changed because you've met someone from there and understand something about their mannerisms, customs, and lives. If students go into the workplace with that understanding already in place, that's how you build partnerships across the company and globally, right?

Teaching these skills with technology requires educators to be mindful of the routines that need to be in place to support the development of 21st-century skills instead of hinder them. Chanmi Chun describes further:

In tech coaching, we need to be mindful of how we are helping students build interpersonal skills with the technology and how to use the technology appropriately in collaborative situations. For example, we need to think about when they should have the technology up and when they should put it to the side. We need teachers to know how to say, "Put your Chromebooks at 45° and listen to me right now." These are ways to help kids learn how to use their technology appropriately during the day.

Learning how to use technology appropriately in collaboration settings and to communicate with one another, is a critical aspect of teaching 21st-century skills in the classroom. When coaches work with teachers to consider the possibilities provided by technology as well as the routines and procedures necessary for success, technology use in the classroom can have powerful effects.

3. *Educational Equity*: A number of education writers have noted that the new fight for educational access and equity is a digital one. In a work world that increasingly requires employees to be competent in the use of technology, having access to opportunities to develop proficiency with that technology in school becomes increasingly critical. According to Future Ready Schools, 21 million US students still lack the broadband capability necessary for digital learning. Further, it is the students who need it the most who lack this access at school and at home.

When educators, districts, and organizations make choices about technology use, they need to consider carefully how students will be able to access the technology and what supports they will need to use it. A lack of mindfulness about access can create a further divide between the haves and the have-nots in schools. Here are a few questions a coach and teachers might need to examine from an equity lens:

◆ Will students be provided with a device or are they asked to bring their own device? How does the answer to this question impact equity of access?

◆ Do all students have access to a device? What can be provided for students who do not have a device?

◆ Are students expected to use that device outside of school? If so, are all students able to access the internet at home? What reasonable options are there for families without internet access?

◆ Does the application you've selected work on all possible devices a student might have?

◆ What assumptions are made about students' technological abilities? How will students receive instruction on the device and/or the application? How will this be differentiated?

Technology has the opportunity to improve opportunities for students or can widen the opportunity gap depending on how it is implemented. Taking into consideration who your students are, their technological needs, and how they access technology as part of instruction is an important conversation for coaches and educators to have when making decisions about edtech use.

Engaging Families with Technology

Transforming the way in which we engage families in our classrooms, schools, and districts is paramount if educators are going to exhaust all options to promote the success of students. A multifaceted approach must be implemented. Families live busy lives and have unique circumstances pertaining to their availability on a given day. Educators must never discount the opportunities that technology provides to a parent or guardian on an internet-enabled device. Grades, learning experiences, event information, feedback, praise, constructive criticism, highlights, and a plethora of other insights can be transmitted to families from educators through a variety of technological methods. Technology coaches can support educators in finding unique ways to leverage social media and digital devices.

So how can technology coaches help educators best engage families in the 21st century? Very simple. Leverage the power of available technology and web applications as a way to connect in the virtual world. Now more than ever, people look to their devices for real-time information. That's why schools must take it upon themselves to activate stakeholder engagement with social media platforms such as Instagram, Pinterest, Facebook, or Twitter. Moving the educational conversation forward and telling your school's story can easily be done in today's world with a few taps of the screen or clicks of the mouse. The technology coach can help their colleagues get started on this digital storytelling initiative by taking an app like Twitter and helping them set up their profile and showing them how to tweet out various learning experiences.

How might this look? Picture a seventh-grade language arts class that is participating in the Global Read Aloud. The teacher takes out his iPhone and captures a great visual of students discussing a book with another class from a different part of the world. The picture, with a brief description and the school hashtag, is then posted to the teacher's Twitter page. Soon thereafter, a parent retweets and includes a little message of how appreciative she is of how the teacher keeps everyone in the loop. Why? Because it enables her to engage in meaningful conversation with her child at the dinner table over what was learned in school that day.

You see, a simple social media post can go a long way in activating family engagement in the school setting. Coupled with an existing amicable relationship, schools can garner more support and strengthen a transparent school culture that is all about promoting the success of students. Utilizing mobile devices, web applications, and a host of other technologies is imperative in today's society. In fact, school stakeholders expect it and would not have it any other way. Technology coaches are the first piece in this puzzle by providing step-by-step instructions on how to use the various features of Twitter.

Other forms of technological hardware can also help keep families engaged with their child's educational experiences. Take, for example, the Swivl that provides users with a hands-free video recording experience. This comes in handy for schools that are hosting events for parents, especially those that might not be able to attend in person. At least once a year, schools will put on a program for parents that speaks to the importance of mental health. There is no doubt that families need exposure to this important topic. On the night of the event, the school guidance counselor sets up the Swivl and records the presentation. Not only was it streamed in real time, but posted on the school website to be viewed by parents at a later date. The technology coach can provide support by researching how the device works and helping set up for whatever educational experience might arise.

The fact of the matter is that educators must be willing to meet families where they currently are in terms of availability and the technology coach can make this process much easier. Some families might be available to experience the presentation, but just not in person. Which is why schools need to find creative ways to provide families with a way to take in the content. Connecting with families in the digital world is along the same lines of providing customers with the option of dining in or taking out. Depending on what is going on with a family's schedule or situation, schools need to find multiple ways for them to experience the products that they are making available. Technology has given the educational world more opportunities to connect with families in ways once thought unimaginable. Now, it's just a matter of putting our collective educational minds together and finding the resources necessary to make these innovative engagement strategies a common reality. Enter the technology coach.

Here are some guiding questions to help with your decision-making process as it relates to what you are trying to accomplish when connecting stakeholders in the virtual world:

◆ Who is my intended audience? (parents, students, staff, community)
◆ What type of message do I want to communicate? (letter, text message, post, flyer)
◆ How do I want to communicate this message? (website, social media, blog, email)
◆ Why do I want to communicate this message? (alert, save the date, helpful information)

Having answers to these questions will make the decision-making process that much easier. For example, if you are celebrating a special classroom or school achievement, then the website might be the way to go. If a coach wants to update the community in real time, then Twitter might be the answer. Finally, if someone wants to remind people to check their email about an important letter regarding school closing, a mass email would work perfectly. There are so many options that instructional coaches could provide colleagues in terms of how to reach the most people with the fewest taps of the screen or clicks of the mouse.

Putting It All Together

Technology by itself will not improve education for students. Teachers must match technology tools with the needs of their students, and apply the tools in pedagogically sound ways that support the development of each student in a holistic way. When done well, the addition of edtech tools can help students develop critical real-world skills and reach levels of learning that might not have been possible without the technology. Providing teachers with an opportunity to explore new technologies that can enhance their instruction in meaningful and aligned ways is the most impactful thing a tech coach can accomplish. We'll end this chapter with a note written by a colleague to Pam Hubler, an instructional coach for the Daniel Island School in Charleston, South Carolina:

> Pam has helped me integrate technology in my classroom effectively. This was an area of both personal and professional growth that has helped me and my students tremendously. Due to my age and lack of experience, she helped me take on the challenge of increasing my knowledge, be open-minded and learn how to use technology more effectively in the classroom. During this time I experienced so much exposure involving hands-on learning with technology and how I can use it in my classroom that built my foundation of knowledge still being used today. I became a better teacher that made lessons and learning more engaging but also helped my students become better learners by increasing their technological skills.

In the next chapter, we will consider how to take the coaching knowledge and skills gained in the first chapters and apply them to the coaching of teams. While similar in some ways, there are additional considerations and skills coaches need to be aware of when planning professional development for groups or working with teams over time. We will look at strategies for making facilitation a success.

References

Alliance for Excellent Education. *Future Ready Schools*. https://futureready.org/about-the-effort/.

Collaborative for Academic, Social, and Emotional Learning. https://casel.org/.

Harris, J.B, Hoffer, M.J., Schmidt, D.A., Blanchard, M.R., Young, C.Y., Grandgenett, N.F., & Van Olphen, M. (2010). "Grounded" technology integration: Instructional planning using curriculum-based activity type taxonomies. *Journal of Technology and Teacher Education, 18*(4), 573–605.

Koehler, M. J. & Mishra, P. (2009). What is technological pedagogical content knowledge? *Contemporary Issues in Technology and Teacher Education, 9*(1), 60–70.

Oberle, E., Domitrovich, C.E., Meyers, D.C., & Weissberg, R.P. (2016). Establishing systemic social and emotional learning approaches in schools: A framework for schoolwide implementation. *Cambridge Journal of Education*, 46(3), 277–297.

Puentedura, R.R. (2006). *Transformation, Technology, and Education*. Retrieved from: http://hippasus.com/resources/tte/.

Sheninger, E. (April 25, 2016). Why pedagogy first, tech second stance is key to the future. *EdTech Magazine*. Retrieved from: https://edtechmagazine.com/k12/article/2016/04/why-pedagogy-first-tech-second-stance-key-future.

Shulman, L.S. (1986). Those who understand: Knowledge growth in teaching. *Educational Researcher*, 15(2), 4–14.

Tucker, C., Wycoff, T., & Green, J.T. (2016). *Blended Learning in Action*. Thousand Oaks, CA: Corwin.

4

Coaching Teams

During your weekly meeting, the principal floats the idea of having you work with grade-level teams to help them consider how technology can support them in meeting their instructional goals. The school is new to working in grade-level teams and, while you have been coaching teachers around tech integration one-on-one, you know that coaching teams or running professional development for the whole staff, will require you to use your current coaching skills in new ways and employ some additional ones as well. Where to start? First, say yes! Then, read this chapter. We'll unpack:

- ◆ the skills required when moving from coaching individuals to coaching teams;
- ◆ the research on the stages of team development and how they impact our work as team developers and facilitators;
- ◆ strategies for helping teams achieve their goals;
- ◆ moves we can make when things go awry in a team meeting; and
- ◆ the three components of keeping a team learning over time.

Moving from Coach to Facilitator

When you coach individuals, the dynamics between the two of you are, generally, easier to manage. You have one person to sleuth out as you tailor your approach to coaching. When you work with a team or are asked to work entire staff, suddenly you are tasked with understanding a group of …duals, their collective strengths and needs, and the dynamics that exist …ween and among the members of the group. Instead of thinking about …ow to help one person achieve their goal, you must support the group in determining a common goal as well as how they will achieve that goal. As a result, your role shifts from coach to facilitator.

A facilitator is really a coach for a group or team. We like the term team because it implies that the group of people you are facilitating are not a group

Figure 4.1 Considerations for Team Facilitators

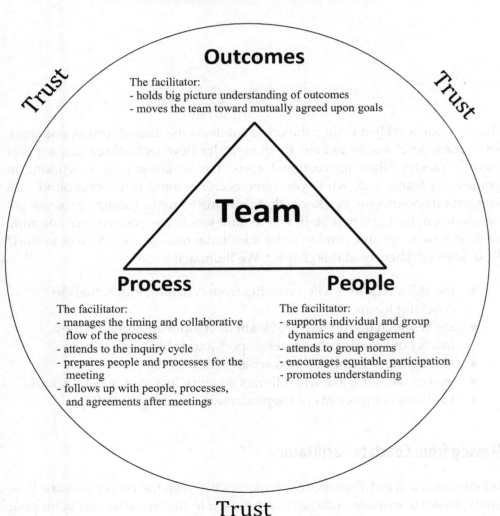

Facilitation Framework

Outcomes

The facilitator:
- holds big picture understanding of outcomes
- moves the team toward mutually agreed upon goals

Team

Process

The facilitator:
- manages the timing and collaborative flow of the process
- attends to the inquiry cycle
- prepares people and processes for the meeting
- follows up with people, processes, and agreements after meetings

People

The facilitator:
- supports individual and group dynamics and engagement
- attends to group norms
- encourages equitable participation
- promotes understanding

Trust

Trust

Trust

of disparate people with little connection to one another. Rather, they are a focused and trained group of professionals working together to achieve a common goal. A team can be as small as two people, or as large as a district staff. As long as they have a common purpose, they can be considered a team. For these reasons, we will use the term team throughout this chapter. In Figure 4.1, the team is in the center. Like a coach, a skilled facilitator works *in service of* the team to accomplish an outcome and knows how to direct the team's energy and processes so the team has emotionally safe and structured ways to engage in important work. There are four variables that facilitators need to consider as they plan work with teams: outcomes, people, process, and trust. Let's explore each component in turn.

1. *Outcomes.* An important role of the facilitator (and any leader really) is to be the vision keeper for the team. A facilitator helps the team stay focused on the reason they are working together and what they hope to accomplish through collaboration. This larger view helps the team create a longer-term plan for achieving their goal, and keeps them from getting lost in the weeds of a particular data set or discussion. It is also the job of the facilitator, therefore, to support the group in making forward progress towards their goal. Facilitators can help the team to clearly articulate and commit to goals and set up agendas (see more below about agendas) that help the group take a series of meaningful steps to achieve those goals. If things get off track, the facilitator can step in and ask the group how the current conversation or decision helps the group move towards their goal and support them in reorienting towards their common goal once more. Maintaining a higher-level understanding and an eye on the long-term plan is a critical for any coach and, particularly, for facilitators of groups.

2. *People.* Knowing how to intentionally foster trusting relationships with individuals and among team members is a critical skill set for effective facilitators. Each member of the team is a unique individual with their own goals, motivations, strengths, needs, and levels of will and skill. Like teachers with a class of students, facilitators need to understand the profile of each member of the team as well as the relational dynamic that exists between and among team members. Further, as the team develops, it will go through several natural stages of development (see more below) that a facilitator must anticipate and take specific and timely actions to address so that the group moves forward in a positive and productive way. This includes setting norms in a way that supports all team members in feeling safe and respected to engage fully,

addressing power dynamics to ensure all members voices are heard and honored, and promoting understanding of a diversity of ideas and opinions in ways that build trust. Building these relationships takes time both inside and outside of team time. Facilitators may need to meet with members ahead of time who express anxiety or frustration, or sit down with others who are showing disengagement after a meeting to address situations (remember your hard conversation skills!). Understanding and intentionally working to develop a team of successful educators is necessary to ensure the whole group is able to work towards the outcomes you have all worked so hard to develop.

3. *Process.* The bridge between outcomes and people is the processes the team undertakes together. Facilitators are tasked with organizing both the logistics (time, space, etc.) as well as considering how to help structure conversations in ways that will help the people achieve the outcomes they desire. Your job is to answer the questions, "How will we get there?" and "What will each step in the process look like?" This can be a short-term process, such as you might create for a one-day professional development, or it might be a longer-term process. Many teams who work together over an extended period of time work through a cycle of inquiry that looks something like this (Figure 4.2):

Figure 4.2 Inquiry Cycle Components

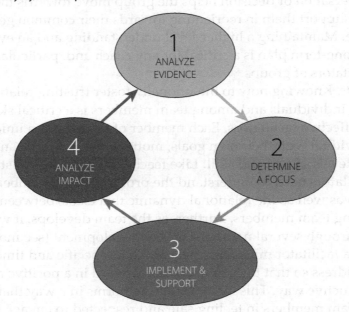

At each stage of the inquiry cycle, the facilitator needs to work with the team to consider what steps need to be taken, how the conversation should flow, what resources might be needed, what collaboration might look like, how much time might be needed, etc. Sometimes protocols are helpful processes to employ at the various stages of the inquiry cycle (see more about protocols below), and the facilitator might work with team members to select specific ones that would help the work move forward productively. In addition, facilitators meet with team members before meetings to prep those who might be sharing data or leading parts of the discussion. They might also meet with team members afterwards to debrief the meeting, follow up on agreements, and support the work in moving forward.

4. *Trust.* Like all endeavors that involve people, nothing real can be done without attending to relationships. As Patrick Lencioni wrote in his 2002 book, *The Five Dysfunctions of a Team*:

> Trust lies at the heart of a functioning, cohesive team. Without it, teamwork is all but impossible. [. . .] trust is the confidence among team members that their peers' intentions are good, and that there is no reason to be protective or careful around the group. In essence, teammates must get comfortable being vulnerable with one another.

(p. 195)

Without trust, teammates will not be able to fully listen to one another, be open to new ideas, take risks, or share their truth with the team. Unless, as Lencioni writes, the team is able to be vulnerable with one another, because they believe their teammates have good intentions, nothing really happens in the group.

Planning Whole Group Professional Development

From time to time a superintendent, principal, or supervisor will ask a tech coach to present about a new technology or innovative method for the entire staff of a team, building, or district. At first this seems like a daunting task, but it's a great opportunity to put your talents as an innovative educator on display. In a weird way, it will help drum up business and give you a chance to connect with each person in the district or school. In addition to keeping in mind the triangle of outcomes, people, and processes we just discussed as you plan your professional development, here are some other helpful tips as you prepare for the big day:

◆ *Follow best practices for planning instruction.*
  ◇ What are your outcomes?
  ◇ How you will know your participants have met those outcomes during instruction at at the end?
  ◇ What instructional activities will help teachers get from where they are now to where you want them to be by the end of your presentation?

◆ *Think about a gradual release learning progression for teaching tech.* In Emily's mentor group, we learned that when introducing new technology to a group, it's best to start by having participants have their tech closed while they watch the presenter use and talk about the tech. Then, you have four choices:
  ◇ Have participants open their tech and follow along step-by-step with time to try each piece and ask questions.
  ◇ Have participants break into small groups or teams to try out the tech with support from more knowledgeable peers.
  ◇ Have participants try the tech individually with support available from more knowledgeable peers.
  ◇ Have all three options available depending on the newness of the tech and the level of tech comfort in the group.

  Make sure you bring the group together again for closure to ensure everyone understands what to do, where to find support, and expectations for next steps.

◆ *Make sure you give participants time to interact* with one another during the presentation. Our general rule of thumb is no more than five-eight minutes of direct instruction before making opportunities for participants to connect, synthesize, and do something with the information you are presenting. Consider using Kagan's Cooperative Learning (2007) strategies to help you design effective interactions. There's even a set designed specifically for trainers.

◆ *Create a slide deck as a set of visuals to accompany your talk.* Be aware of having too many words on a slide as brain research shows those listening to your presentation cannot read and listen to you at the same time. They can, however, look at images and look at you! Make sure you share out your presentation so that people can refer back to it at a later time.

◆ *Practice your presentation with particular attention to transitions and timing.* Consider how you will get your materials to people as well as how you will get their attention. Get another set of eyes on your materials and presentation prior to the big day.

◆ *Highlight some of the great work you are doing with colleagues.* Everyone appreciates a shout-out every now and again.

◆ *Share personal stories* at the beginning, middle, and end of the professional development so that you can really show people that you are human and truly appreciate the great work of educators.

◆ *Ask for feedback from participants and colleagues* about your presentation. This is how you learn and grow as a presenter!

◆ Finally, *be yourself*, everyone else is already taken!

Whether you are working with a small team over time, or working with a larger group once, let's talk about how teams form and some of the tools tech coaches-turned-facilitators can use to develop trust, build relationships with people, and select effective processes to achieve desired outcomes.

It's Not Just Your Team: Moving through the Stages of Group Development

If you are working with a team over time, it's important to understand and prepare for the way teams change. As teams develop, form, and work together over time, they naturally go through a series of developmental periods. In 1965, psychology professor, Bruce Tuckman, first described four stages of group development— forming, storming, norming, and performing—that all groups naturally go through.

In the **forming** stage, the newly formed group expresses confusion and uncertainty about their work together. They test out each other, the rules of the group, and the roles and power dynamics of the team members as they get acquainted. They begin to define goals for their work together, but generally look outside the group or to a group leader for guidance and direction. Little is actually accomplished during this phase as a result of the anxiety and unsureness felt by the members of the team.

Teams move from forming to **storming**. As the group begins to understand team dynamics and, perhaps, to zero in on what they need to do together, disagreements arise. This phase is sometimes marked by struggles over priorities and/or leadership. Some team members may not like the direction the group is headed and look for reasons to disengage, reject the work of the group, or seek to undermine the leader of the group. While there is still a lot of uncertainty about expressing individual opinions or ideas, cliques may form causing conflict, tension, or even open hostility.

Groups that pass through the storming phase find themselves in the **norming** period of group development. This stage is marked by a move towards consensus and acceptance of leadership as trust is established, standards are set, and roles are determined within the group. The team grows more cohesive in their work and focused on the task at hand. Processes and procedures are developed to deal with the task, and ideas begin to be expressed more openly as the team builds confidence in themselves and the work.

Finally, groups move into the **performing** stage. The main concern of teams in this stage is getting the job done. Processes are in place to ensure objectives are achieved, people are focused on their common goal, communicate effectively, are able to solve problems as they arise, and are generally more flexible in their roles within the group. There is generally a sense of openness and helpfulness. It is only at this stage of team development that teams reach a period of high performance.

All teams must go through these stages as they develop. How long or short each phase lasts depends a great deal on the members of the team as well as the leader of the team (the facilitator or coach). While teams generally move from forming to performing in a linear fashion, there are times during which a team may backslide from performing to storming over a difficult issue and then need to work themselves back through norming to performing again. Some groups, on the other hand, may get stuck in the forming or storming stage and never move forward into the more productive phases of teamwork.

The amount of time it takes to complete this cycle varies greatly based on a number of factors including frequency and duration of meetings, clarity of outcomes, engagement and stability of team members, leadership both within the group and external, and the nature of the group's activities. However, some teams never complete the cycle at all. Some teams never get beyond the forming stage. While they may be polite to one another, all that head nodding does not translate into actual work. Many teams accept that storming is a normal way of operating and so, as a result, spend their time together complaining or unpacking all the reasons why something won't work for them. Some teams fail to norm fully and, so, any challenge that arises amongst team members creates a degeneration into storming due to lack of trust or necessary processes.

As you read this, you may find yourself thinking back to teams of which you have been a member. We have all, at one time or another, found ourselves on a team that was painful to be part of as well as on teams that performed extraordinarily well. Perhaps, as you review these stages, you can think of specific things members of the team or leaders did that allowed the team to move forward towards performing or held the group back in one of the developmental stages. It wasn't just your team! And, as a coach, you can help your team to do better. Coaches can use this knowledge of how teams develop to help the group plan for success. For example, noticing that the group is fighting the task and exhibiting passive aggressive behaviors can alert the coach that the team is stuck in the storming phase. The coaching might create opportunities for the team to reconnect with their broader mission and with one another in ways that help bring them back to the group. Another example might be when a savvy facilitator notices that the group is norming and decides to spend time on developing team norms and introducing protocols that allow team members to participate in productive conversations that are structured and safe. These deliberate actions on the part of the facilitator can support the development of trust and, therefore, a willingness of the team members to move more quickly into the performing stage.

Harnessing the knowledge of how groups develop and what is needed at each stage of their development can empower a coach to plan work with the team in ways that support movement from forming to performing in the shortest and most positive way possible.

Adding to Your Coaching Tool Kit: Strategies for Moving Forward Together

Now that you've got a sense of what your role is in coaching a group or facilitating a larger team, and a better understanding of the natural stages teams go through when they form, let's explore three additional strategies you can use to help your team progress positively together. These strategies are: setting norms, building effective agendas, and harnessing the power of protocols. These are proactive strategies that, when attended to ahead of meetings, can set your group up for success.

1. Setting Norms
Whether stated or left unspoken, all teams, regardless of size, develop accepted ways of work or "norms." Some of these ways of work are healthier than others. Some norms privilege certain members of the group—they are part of the dominant culture, have a position of authority, or are more outspoken—but these same norms are less positive and, perhaps, even threatening, for other members of the group. A savvy facilitator, therefore, will work with the team to generate a set of agreements purposefully in ways that are inclusive of all voices and to set the tone for how the group will operate from the beginning. To be clear, when we say "norms," we mean:

a. agreements generated by the team;
b. intended for all team members to uphold;
c. aligned with the function and context of the team;
d. subject to change and refinement as the team's development or task changes; and
e. revisited regularly as needed.

Norms are *not*:

a. rules for the facilitator to create and enforce;
b. rules for the administrator to create and enforce, nor are they;
c. always transferable from one working team to another.

In other words, norms define the unique culture of the team in ways that are clear and acceptable to all members of the team.

For some people and teams, the word "norm" is loaded with negative context for one reason or another. Feel free to substitute the term for something more appropriate in your context such as, "ways of work," "working agreements," or "team agreements."

Some have asked whether norms (or whatever you have decided to call them) are needed for all groups. We answer that with a resounding, yes! Whether your group is small or large, all groups have a culture of work that can be improved by stating what members of the group need. Without them, members of the team operate on an assumption that all people need the same things from the group as they do. In very small and large teams, in teams that meet daily or only quarterly, or even once, norms can help keep a group be focused on what is important, stay on track as a team, and provide clarity about what to do when there are challenges. They provide a third point to which all members of the group can point and say, these are the things we agreed upon. How are are living up to those agreements?

Let's talk about what kind of norms effective teams generally create for themselves. Most have norms that include some version of these five components:

a. respect and sensitivity in comments;
b. maintain non-judgmental attitude;
c. encourage evidence-based conversation;
d. expectation that all contribute to substantive/forward-moving conversation; and
e. commitment to staying within allotted time.

Each of these categories defines a way of working together that is positive, assumes responsibility by all members of the team, and is focused on the task. Below (Figure 4.3) are four sets of norms from real teams.

Take a look again at these norms. What do you notice about them? You might notice that they are phrased positively—they describe what the team *will* do instead of what it *will not* do. They are also few in number, ranging between three and five norms in total. As a set, they each define clear cultural values and ways of work for these unique teams. What might the norms look like in your group?

Figure 4.3 Norm Examples

• Start and end on time • Be fully present (no sidebars, grading papers) • Disagree agreeably	• Attack issues, not people • What goes on here, stays here • Come prepared • Follow through
• Maintain confidentiality • Attend to self and others • Listen to understand • Assume positive intentions	• Presume positive intentions • Probe for specificity • Put ideas on the table • Pay attention to self and others • Pursue a balance between advocacy and inquiry

If you are working with a team once, you may want to come with a set of generic norms for your presentation. It is not worth the time to co-create norms in this situation. However, if your team will meet multiple times, you will need to help your team develop norms for themselves. Thinking back to the triangle of facilitator responsibilities, the process for norm setting needs to take into consideration the outcomes of the team, the people on the team, and determining a process you use to get those people to those outcomes all wrapped up in a trusting atmosphere. Below is a process Emily teaches facilitators to use with their teams. As you review the steps, consider what this might look like and sound like with your team. What would you need to consider, say, or do at each step to help your people meet your collective outcomes?

1. Facilitator shares the purpose and benefits of using norms. "Our goal is to establish agreements for our team so we can be productive, equitable, and safe in our work together."
2. Ask team members to consider behaviors they feel are necessary for their team to have a professional and productive meeting. The facilitator might share example norms (think about the broad categories or the four sets of sample norms listed above). Encourage them to think about norms that represent positive behaviors, not negative ones.
3. Provide two-three large Post-its and a marker to each team member. Have them write one norm on each of their Post-its.
4. Have team members each take turns reading one of their norms. As the team member reads their norm, have them place their Post-it either on chart paper or on a whiteboard.
5. As other team members shares a norm, ask the team to determine whether that norm is similar to another norm already posted or different. Affinity group the Post-its so all team members can see. It is fine at this stage to have many groups. It is more important that all team members feel their ideas are being heard and valued.

6. Once all team members have shared their norms, invite the team to review the groupings and ask any clarifying questions of one another regarding the meaning of norms. This is a critical stage as the team is working to develop a common understanding.

7. Ask the team the best way to state each norm suggested by the Post-its in a particular group. Do NOT write anything down until there is agreement amongst all team members about how to phrase a particular norm. Once there is agreement, write out the language of that norm. Repeat for remaining groupings.

8. Once all norm language is determined, the facilitator confirms with the group that these are the right set of norms for this team and confirms that all team members are able to adhere to the proposed norms. Invite clarification of thinking and feelings. Remind the team that norms are not set in stone and that you will regularly revisit them as a team and can decide to add, delete, and adjust norms at any point.

9. Debrief the process with the team. What worked? What was challenging/raised concerns?

10. After the meeting, create a poster or otherwise record the final version of the norms in a location all team members can see and access.

11. Remember to post norms in some way at all meetings and take time to review them regularly during future meetings.

Using your well-developed coaching language and stances during this process is critical to the success of the norm-setting process. It is critical that all members of the team feel heard and equally valued in this situation. Model good paraphrasing, ask clarifying questions, offer invitational suggestions, and be patient with the team as they work to develop common meaning. This is not an easy process! However, if done well, it will go a long way towards building trust amongst the members of your team and creating ways of work that will see you through more challenging times as the group moves forward together.

Many people ask about the timing of this process. When should you go about forming norms? Is this something you do right way when a team first comes together? What if a team has been meeting for a long time? Do we need to recreate norms when a new member joins? Our general rule is that norms are something that should be considered early in the forming process of team development because they help the team move through the storming phase more quickly and less painfully. That being said, we don't suggest you jump into norm setting as the very first item of business for your team either. Take some time to get to know one another and get clear about your structure and task first. This will allow you and the members of your team to take stock of one another, notice natural ways of work within the team (for better or worse), and think about what each member of the team will need from this team in order to accomplish the collective goal. We do encourage you not to wait too long before creating norms, however. If you wait until the team is in the storming phase of development when distrust and confusion are at their peak, norm creation can become a venue for some members of the team to punish others. (i.e. "I think we need a norm about being on time because Kenny is always late."). As you can imagine, trying to create norms under these circumstances can have the opposite impact on team morale and trust.

If, on the other hand, you have a team that has been meeting for a long time, has a clearly established set of norms and a positive culture of work already, you may not need to start from scratch with norm development. As we've mentioned before, norms are less about what is written on the paper, and more about what the group understands the norms to mean for this team. So, when new members join, as well as periodically with any group, it is a good idea to revisit the norms. This could include taking time to define what they mean or having team members share what they believe the norms mean for the group and what they look or sound like in action. It could also mean making decisions about whether you need to keep all the norms you currently have, or whether there are some norms you no longer need, or ones that might be beneficial to add. Taking the time to define norms, to discuss what they mean, their implications for the work, and what they look like when enacted well helps all teams to develop a common vision of successful team interactions and language to talk about those interactions over time.

To recap, norms can be powerful for groups of all sizes, makeups, and foci. They work best when they are co-created in a meaningful way and before the group hits the storming stage. They can be maintained most easily by making them live in each meeting. This can be accomplished by posting them regularly, referring to them often, reflecting on the group's success in living those norms in each meeting, discussing their evolving and deepening meaning over time, and adjusting them as necessary. With a living set of norms in place that all stakeholders own, great work can be done by the team even when things get challenging.

2. Building Effective Agendas

Every meeting you've ever been to has probably had an agenda of some kind, so what's the big deal, right? While it is true that most meetings are guided by some kind of agenda, they generally miss the opportunity that agendas can provide to help structure and guide a meeting as well as create a historical record for the group over time. In our experience, the most powerful agendas include the following items:

    a.   the date, time, and location;
    b.   clear outcomes;
    c.   the team norms;
    d.   roles for meeting participants;
    e.   times for each item on the agenda;
    f.   processes for how decisions will be made;
    g.   a place for notes and agreements made during the meeting;
    h.   space to talk about next steps, time frames, and responsibilities; and
    i.   space for team members to provide feedback on the meeting and input on the agenda for the next meeting.

Below are two sample agendas (Figures 4.4 and 4.5). As you review them, note the presence of the nine items listed above. How are they included in the agenda? How might these pieces collectively improve the quality of a meeting?

This first sample is of an agenda that might be created for the first time a team meets together. There is a clear date, time, and location listed at the top and a place for the norms to be included once they are created in the norms section of the agenda. There are clear topics for discussion as well as purpose statements for each topic to support team members in understanding the goal for that section. Some sections further include bulleted items that provide discussion topics or steps within that section that need to be addressed. There are also clear time frames for each section so everyone is clear in advance the amount of time available for each section. On the right side of the agenda is a place for the group to record outcomes—decision points and agreements that the team wants to remember. As this is a first meeting, there are no set roles for team members yet, however, this concept is introduced in the logistics section of the agenda. At the end of the agenda, there is time for the team to review decisions, confirm next steps, and discuss the next agenda as well as to provide public feedback on the meeting's structures and progress towards goals.

Having an agenda like this in place from the first time the team convenes sets up a positive and transparent culture for how the team will work together, what the team will do, how decisions will be made, and how follow-through will be ensured. The content of this agenda focuses squarely on building relationships, clarifying the work, and setting up processes for successful group interaction.

This second sample agenda could be taken from any time in the middle of the year after a group has begun its work together. It could also serve as an agenda for a team that meets only once. As you review it, you might see indicators of a team in the performing phase of development. Like the first agenda, there is a place at the top for date, time, and location

Figure 4.4 Sample Agenda 1: First Team Meeting of the Year

Date:	Norms (TBD):
Time:	
Location:	
Team Members Present:	
Team Members Absent:	

Time	Topics/Notes	Outcomes
10 mins.	**Introductions/Connector** **Purpose:** *To connect as a team around our hopes for collaborative work*	
5 mins.	**Opening** **Purpose:** *To provide an overview of our time together* • Share outcomes • Review agenda	
30 mins.	**Defining Team Purpose** **Purpose:** *To clarify with the team the goals of this team; to consider both short- and long-term desired outcomes*	
30 mins.	**Norms** **Purpose:** *To use a protocol to identify team norms to ensure productive, equitable, and safe meetings*	
10 mins.	**Logistics** **Purpose:** *To discuss details related to how the meetings will be run and information shared* • Reviews dates/times/places for meetings • Roles for team members (facilitator, recorder, timekeeper, snacks) • Methods for sharing agendas, notes, other information • Other	
30 mins.	**Beginning a Discussion about A Team Inquiry Question** **Purpose:** *To brainstorm/discuss current student learning needs and what data the team needs for the next meeting in order to determine a team inquiry question connected with the team's stated purpose*	
10 mins.	**Closure** **Purpose:** *To review progress made towards outcomes and discuss next meeting outcomes and agenda items. Confirm next meeting date and what to bring (student work, assessment data)* • Review outcomes • Discuss next meeting outcomes and agenda • Confirm next meeting date and what to bring	
10 mins.	**Feedback (+/Δ)** **Purpose:** *To provide time for members to discuss successes and challenges related to the meeting process to improve future meetings, and capture learning on inquiry cycle content* • Process: How did it go? What worked? What was less successful today? (norms, facilitation, team dev.) • Content: What did we do/learn?	

Figure 4.5 Sample Agenda 2: Ongoing Meeting Agenda

Date: Time: Location: Timekeeper: Sandra Recorder: Lin Snack Provider: Reina	Norms: Start and end on time Come prepared Be fully present Assume positive intent Use data to drive the work

Time/ Facilitator	Topics	Purpose/Outcome	Agreements/ Responsible People
10 mins. Chris	**Connector**	*To build relationships and reconnect team members to each other and the work*	
5 mins. Sandra	**Opening** • Outcomes • Agenda • Norms	*To make team aware of the outcomes, get feedback on the agenda, and revisit norms to ensure a productive, equitable and safe meeting*	

50 mins.
Ben
	Inquiry Cycle
	• Analyze and Reflect
	  ○ use looking at student data protocol to analyze work brought by all members of the team in connection with team goal
	  ○ determine student strengths and needs
	  ○ notice data patterns that could lead to instructional shifts
	  ○ brainstorm next steps based on data
		To engage in an ongoing cycle of inquiry to improve the quality of teaching and learning	

5 mins. Reina	**Next Steps** • Clarify team agreements: Who? What? When? How?	*To ensure all members are aware of team agreements and clarify any questions*	
10 min. Lin	**Closure** • Review progress on meeting outcomes • Discuss next meeting outcomes and agenda • Confirm next meeting date and what to bring	*To review progress made towards outcomes and discuss next meeting outcomes and agenda. Confirm next meeting date and what to bring (student work, assessments)*	
10 min. Brian	**Feedback (+/Δ)** • Process: How did it go? What worked? What was less successful today? (norms, facilitation, team dev.) • Content: What did we do/learn about . . .? ○ instruction, assessment, students, our inquiry	*To provide an opportunity for members to discuss successes and challenges related to the meeting process to improve future PLCs, and capture learning on inquiry cycle content*	

of the meeting. Roles have been established for team members, and are listed at the top and down the left side of the agenda. Notice that a number of different team members' names are listed. This suggests the team has moved into that performing phase where there is shared leadership and facilitation occuring. Norms are also clearly listed at the top of the agenda. While organized slightly differently from the first example, this agenda also includes clear items for discussion and purpose statements as well as times allotted to each section. There is a place for the recorder to capture agreements and responsible parties on the far right as well. Closure and feedback are also included and given sufficient time at the end of the meeting. This meeting agenda includes a place for team members to work through a piece of the inquiry cycle-analysis. You will note team members are each tasked with bringing data to share. Another indicator that this team has moved into a phase of buy-in, openness, and willingness to share.

This agenda continues to make space for the team to connect with one another while focusing clearly on the work the team is undertaking. It is goal focused with clear processes and shared responsibility in place. Having this kind of agenda supports a functioning team in continuing to remain focused and functional.

Savvy facilitators understand the power of a well-structured agenda. It is helpful both in developing teams that have a culture of focused collaboration and helping teams to maintain their focus and process as they progress in their work together. It is also important to note that agendas are most effective when they are sent out well before the meeting. Knowing ahead of time what to expect and what is expected of each team member helps everyone come to the table ready to participate. Agendas also need to be shared during the meeting—posted, distributed on paper, or shared electronically—so all can view it and be clear about how the meeting will progress. A clear agenda built with input from team members and shared in advance is a powerful preventative coaching measure that can truly help teams to work well together.

3. Harnessing the Power of Protocols

You may have noticed as you reviewed the sample agendas in the previous section that some included a set of steps for how a team would work through a specific item on an agenda. These steps or "protocols" are the third powerful preventative tool in a facilitator's kit. We like to think of protocols as guardrails on the highway to success. Guardrails on a freeway provide clear boundaries for drivers. They help drivers stay in their lanes of travel and know where it is acceptable to drive as they move down the road. Protocols do the same things in meetings. They create a transparent process for all team members. They clarify what will happen and when and create safety through that predictability. Take a moment to review the chart below (Figure 4.6) which describes what protocols can provide for a team and what happens, in

Figure 4.6 The Power of Protocols in Meetings

In meetings using protocols	In some meetings not using protocols
There is clearly defined space for active listening and silent reflection	Participants speak over one another, jump in to speak, speak without thinking first, and digress from the focus frequently
Equity and parity are emphasized and valued so all voices will be heard	Few voices doing most talking, others are silent or silenced, and many participants feel distant or disengaged from the team
Participants feel safe to ask difficult questions and give/receive honest feedback	People feel attacked or abused
The focus is on the work and there is a genuine attempt to address and resolve any challenges or dilemmas that arise	Significant defensiveness and "us vs. them" mentality may arise
Participants gain perspectives and leave feeling empowered, optimistic, and with actionable next steps	Frequent bickering, endless complaining about the same problems over and over, stonewalling, or defeated silence may occur
	People leave the meeting without clear next steps or much hope for progress

some instances, when protocols are not in place. Think about your team and how protocols might help them to take steps towards the kind of trusting, open, collaborative, and focused group you want them to become or remain:

Protocols are really just a set of steps a team uses to make progress towards a goal. They can be short or long, highly detailed or looser in nature. There are literally thousands of protocols posted free online for facilitators to use.[1]

The question then becomes, how do you go about selecting a protocol for your team that would be helpful? It is easy to get lost in all of the possibilities. The best advice we can offer is to go back to the triangle of outcomes–people—process. A protocol is a process. You need, therefore, to think about how to select a process that is going to help your people get to their outcome. In some instances, it might also be helpful to think about the stages of the inquiry cycle as you select a protocol. For example, if your team needs to be more grounded in data before making a decision about how to proceed, a protocol that helps the team to look at student work would be beneficial. If your team is trying something new in their classrooms and is getting stuck, a student observation protocol might be most useful. In Figure 4.7 below, we have recreated that inquiry cycle with the titles of some protocols from the School Reform Initiative free list that might be an interesting place to start:

Let's look at one protocol here as an example (Figure 4.8). As you review it, notice how it is structured. What are the steps in the process? What is the role of the facilitator in the process? What are participants asked to do or not do during each step? When in a team's work might this protocol be useful? What would this protocol help your team to accomplish?

Figure 4.7 Inquiry Cycle-Aligned Protocols

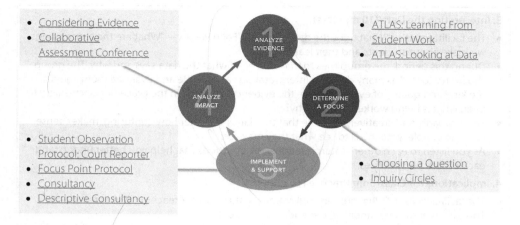

Figure 4.8 ATLAS Looking at Data Protocol

ATLAS

Looking at Data

Learning from Data is a tool to guide groups of teachers discovering what students, educators, and the public understand and how they are thinking. The tool, developed by Eric Buchovecky, is based in part on the work of the Leadership for Urban Mathematics Project and the Assessment Communities of Teachers Project. The tool also draws on the work of Steve Seidel and Evangeline Harris-Stefanakis of Project Zero at Harvard University. Revised November 2000 by Gene Thompson-Grove. Revised August 2004 for Looking at Data by Dianne Leahy.

1. Getting Started

- The facilitator reminds the group of the norms.
- The educator providing the data set gives a very brief statement of the data and avoids explaining what she/he concludes about the data if the data belongs to the group rather than the presenter.

Note: Each of the next 4 steps should be about 10 minutes in length. It is sometimes helpful for the facilitator to take notes.

2. Describing the Data (10 minutes)

- The facilitator asks: "What do you see?"
- During this period the group gathers as much information as possible from the data.
- Group members describe what they see in data, avoiding judgments about quality or interpretations.
- It is helpful to identify where the observation is being made—e.g., "On page one in the second column, third row . . ."
- If judgments or interpretations do arise, the facilitator should ask the person to describe the evidence on which they are based.
- It may be useful to list the group's observations on chart paper. If interpretations come up, they can be listed in another column for later discussion during Step 3.

(continued)

Figure 4.8 *(continued)*

3. Interpreting the Data (10 minutes)

- The facilitator asks: "What does the data suggest?" Followed by—"What are the assumptions we make about students and their learning?"
- During this period, the group tries to make sense of what the data says and why. The group should try to find as many different interpretations as possible and evaluate them against the kind and quality of evidence. From the evidence gathered in the preceding section, try to infer: what is being worked on and why?
- Think broadly and creatively. Assume that the data, no matter how confusing, makes sense to some people; your job is to see what they may see.
- As you listen to each other's interpretations, ask questions that help you better understand each other's perspectives.

4. Implications for Classroom Practice (10 minutes)

- The facilitator asks: "What are the implications of this work for teaching and assessment?" This question may be modified, depending on the data.
- Based on the group's observations and interpretations, discuss any implications this work might have for teaching and assessment in the classroom. In particular, consider the following questions:

    o What steps could be taken next?
    o What strategies might be most effective?
    o What else would you like to see happen? What kinds of assignments or assessments could provide this information?
    o What does this conversation make you think about in terms of your own practice? About teaching and learning in general?
    o What are the implications for equity?

5. Reflecting on the ATLAS-Looking at Data (10 minutes)
Presenter Reflection:

- What did you learn from listening to your colleagues that was interesting or surprising?
- What new perspectives did your colleagues provide?
- How can you make use of your colleagues' perspectives?

Group Reflection:

- What questions about teaching and assessment did looking at the data raise for you?
- Did questions of equity arise?
- How can you pursue these questions further?
- Are there things you would like to try in your classroom as a result of looking at this data?

6. Debrief the Process (5 minutes)

- How well did the process work?
- What about the process helped you to see and learn interesting or surprising things?
- What could be improved?

Reproduced by permission from the author, Dianne Leahy

You may have noticed that this protocol is quite short—the suggested time is less than 50 minutes in length, making it a good fit for most team meeting times. The team progresses through a set of steps in which they review and discuss the the data in different ways. First, they review on their own, then they describe the data, then they interpret the data. Having these as separate steps helps the team to keep from jumping immediately to conclusions about the data. Only after these steps are accomplished does the team move into discussing implications for classroom practice. There is even time for debriefing the protocol built into this example. In each step, there is a clear role for the facilitator including example questions the facilitator might ask and what to do and look out for in each step. There are also clear roles for participants. The acceptable responses in each section are defined clearly. This helps all members of the team know what to expect from each other and provides clarity about what they can say in each section. As this is an analysis of student data, it would fit well during the analyzing evidence or impact phases of the inquiry cycle. Protocols like this one could help your team to get grounded in the data so that they can think about how to move forward in a data-driven way.

Protocols can also be helpful when a team gets stuck and needs help figuring out how to move forward again. We like the consultancy protocol

Figure 4.9 Consultancy Protocol

Consultancy Protocol

Framing Consultancy Dilemmas

Developed by Faith Dunne, Paula Evans, and Gene Thompson-Grove as part of their work at the Coalition of Essential Schools and the Annenberg Institute for School Reform.

Purpose

The structure of the Consultancy helps presenters think more expansively about a particular, concrete dilemma. The Consultancy protocol has 2 main purposes—to develop participants' capacity to see and describe the dilemmas that are the essential material of their work, and to help each other understand and deal with them.

Framing Consultancy Dilemmas and Consultancy Questions

A dilemma is a puzzle: an issue that raises questions, an idea that seems to have conceptual gaps, or something about process or product that you just can't figure out. All dilemmas have some sort of identifiable tension in them. Sometimes the dilemma will include samples of student or adult work that illustrate it, but often the dilemma crosses over many parts of the educational process.

1. Think About Your Dilemma

Dilemmas deal with issues with which you are struggling or that you are unsure about. Some questions or helping you select a dilemma might include:

- Is it something that is bothering you enough that your thoughts regularly return to it?
- Is it something that is not already on its way to being resolved?
- Is it something that does not depend on getting other people to change—in other words, can you affect the dilemma by changing your practice?
- Is it something that is important to you, and is it something you are willing to work on?

2. Do Some Reflective Writing About Your Dilemma

- Some questions that might help are:
- Why is this a dilemma for you? Why is this dilemma important to you?
- What (or where) is the tension in your dilemma?

(continued)

Figure 4.9 *(continued)*

- If you could take a snapshot of this dilemma, what would you/we see?
- What have you done already to try to remedy or manage the dilemma?
- What have been the results of those attempts?
- Who needs to change? Who needs to take action to resolve this dilemma? If your answer is not you, you need to change your focus. You will want to present a dilemma that is about your practice, actions, behaviors, beliefs, and assumptions, and not someone else's.
- What do you assume to be true about this dilemma, and how have these assumptions influenced your thinking about the dilemma?
- What is your focus question? A focus question summarizes your dilemma and helps focus the feedback.

3. Frame a Focus Question for Your Consultancy Group

- Try to pose a question around the dilemma that seems to you to get to the heart of the matter.
- Remember that the question you pose will guide the Consultancy group in their discussion of the dilemma.

4. Critique Your Focus Question

- Is this question important to my practice?
- Is this question important to student learning?
- Is this question important to others in my profession?

Some Generic Examples of Dilemmas—with framing questions

- My teaching team seems to love the idea of involving students in meaningful learning that connects students to real issues and an audience beyond school, but nothing seems to be happening in reality.
- Question: *What can I do to capitalize on my team's interest, so we can translate theory into practice?*
- No matter how hard I try to be inclusive and ask for everyone's ideas, about half of the people don't want to do anything new—they think things were just fine before.
- Question: *How do I work with the people who don't want to change without alienating them?*
- I am completely committed to the value of play for children's learning in my early
- childhood classroom, but often feel pressured to spend more and more time on academic work.
- Question: *How do I incorporate play into my 1st grade classroom, while keeping the demands of the academic curriculum in mind?*

Preparing to Present using the Consultancy Protocol

Come to the session with a description of a dilemma related to your practice. Write your dilemma with as much contextual description as you feel you need for understanding. One page is generally sufficient; even a half page is often enough. If you prefer not to write it out, you can make notes for yourself and do an oral presentation, but please do some preparation ahead of time.

- End your description with a specific question. Frame your question thoughtfully. What do you REALLY want to know? What is your real dilemma? Name the tension(s) in the framing question. This question will help your Consultancy group focus its feedback. Questions that can be answered with a "yes" or "no" generally provide less feedback for the person with the dilemma, so avoid those kinds of questions.

Note: *See Consultancy Protocol to process dilemmas.*

Consultancy Protocol

Purpose

- The structure of the Consultancy helps presenters think more expansively about a particular, concrete dilemma. The Consultancy protocol has 2 main purposes—to develop participants' capacity to see and describe the dilemmas that are the essential material of their work, and to help each other understand and deal with them.

Time: Approximately 50 minutes

Roles

- Presenter (whose work is being discussed by the group)
- Facilitator (who sometimes participates, depending on the size of the group)
- Consultants

Outside perspective is critical to the effectiveness of this protocol; therefore, some of the participants in the group should be people who do not share the presenter's specific dilemma at that time. The Consultancy group is typically a small and intimate one—from 4–7 people. Larger groups can easily be subdivided into consultancy groups.

- **Process**

1. The presenter gives an overview of the dilemma with which she/he is struggling, and frames a question for the consultancy group to consider. The framing of this question, as well as the quality of the presenter's reflection on the dilemma being discussed, are key features of this protocol. If the presenter has brought student work, educator work, or other "artifacts," there is a pause here to silently examine the work/documents. The focus of the group's conversation is on the dilemma. (10–15 minutes if there are artifacts to examine)

2. The consultancy group asks clarifying questions of the presenter—that is, questions that have brief, factual answers. (5 minutes)

3. The group asks probing questions of the presenter (See Pocket Guide to Probing Questions). These questions should be worded so that they help the presenter clarify and expand her/ his thinking about the dilemma presented to the consultancy group. The goal here is for the presenter to learn more about the question she/he framed and to do some analysis of the dilemma presented. The presenter responds to the group's questions, although sometimes a probing question might ask the presenter to see the dilemma in such a novel way that the response is simply, "I never thought about it that way." There is no discussion by the consultancy group of the presenter's responses. At the end of the 10 minutes, the facilitator asks the presenter to restate her/his question for the group. (10 minutes)

4. The group talks with each other about the dilemma presented. In this step, the group works to define the issues more thoroughly and objectively. Sometimes members of the group suggest actions the presenter might consider taking; if they do, these should be framed as "open suggestions," and should be made only after the group has thoroughly analyzed the dilemma. The presenter doesn't speak during this discussion, but listens in and takes notes. The group talks about the presenter in the third person. (15 minutes)

Possible questions to frame the discussion:

- What did we hear?
- What didn't we hear that might be relevant?
- What assumptions seem to be operating?
- What questions does the dilemma raise for us?
- What do we think about the dilemma?
- What might we do or try if faced with a similar dilemma? What have we done in similar situations?

5. The presenter reflects on what she/he heard and on what she/he is now thinking, sharing with the group anything that particularly resonated for him or her during any part of the Consultancy. (5 minutes)

6. The facilitator leads a brief conversation about the group's observation of the Consultancy process.
   (5 minutes)

Note: *See Consultancy Dilemmas to craft dilemmas for use with the Consultancy Protocol and Facilitation Tips for process advice.*

for situations like this because there are very clear stages to the discussion and roles for participants that support the team in slowing down their process, engaging in new thinking, and getting unstuck. Take a look at the consultancy protocol in Figure 4.9. How might a protocol such as this help your team?

As stated in the protocol, the purpose of this process is both to help the presenter of the dilemma to be clear about the issue, and to help others understand the issue so that they can work together to resolve it. The success of this protocol hangs on the development of the initial dilemma and how it is framed to the group. Facilitators will need to work closely with presenters to make sure they are set up for success from the beginning. If set up well, the questioning and the discussion often lead to incredible insights and ideas that can help both the presenter and the team as a whole to move forward in new and exciting ways generated by the collective brainpower of the team. We generally find that this protocol has another positive side effect—through this process, teams often build respect for one another and increase their willingness to risk take with one another in ways that build and deepen trust.

In this section we have explored two of our favorite protocols of the thousands that are available. Generally, most facilitators and teams end up adopting a small handful of protocols they like and use them frequently. However, it is sometimes a good idea to mix it up and try a new protocol when you want to change the energy of the team or want to inspire new thinking and ideas.

Some people shy away from implementing protocols because they can feel awkward at first. The specificity of the steps, the requirements for specific types of actions or responses at certain points in the process can feel uncomfortable at first. That uncomfortableness is felt most keenly by those whose voices may have been loudest in previous settings or who have grown used to teams that are stuck in the storming phase. Protocols can help teams norm (or renorm) around ways of work that are healthy and productive for all members of the team. Over time, as the group begins to internalize some of these protocols, facilitators can loosen the structures of the protocol, adapt protocols, or even make up new protocols that better fit the way a team is working. However, regardless of where in the development cycle a team is, protocols are always useful.

In this section, we've explored three new facilitation strategies you can use to help your team work positively together: setting norms, building effective agendas, and harnessing the power of protocols. These proactive team coaching strategies can set your team up for success from the beginning, if employed in thoughtful ways. However, even when you do your best work to set your team up for success, sometimes things don't go exactly to plan. In the next section, we will talk about some coaching interventions you can enact to help get your team back on track.

Something's Not Right: Productively Addressing Team Challenges

> The tech coach has been asked by the principal to run a workshop for each department on web applications that pump out real-time data to drive future discussion. She has worked very hard on the presentation and is looking forward to a wonderful few hours of learning. As team members are walking in, the tech coach overhears one of her colleagues making negative comments about the "required" workshop. He comments on how technology never works in his classroom and is, quite frankly, overwhelmed with the whole prospect of planning a lesson or unit of study around a website or app. During the three-hour long workshop, he is seen dozing off, browsing the internet, and grading papers. The tech coach tries at various points to provide assistance and motivate her colleague to stay focused. Even though the workshop as a whole was well received, the tech coach could not get over the fact that this colleague would act so unprofessionally.

We've all had the unfortunate experience of being part of a team meeting that didn't go well. Take a moment and think back to one of those challenging meetings. What made it challenging? How did you feel? Most of us immediately recall feelings of stress or anger when recalling those situations. Even if you have done all the things we have described in the first part of this chapter—created norms, organized clear agendas, and employed structured protocols—sometimes things happen during team meetings that can take even the most productive team off track. In this section, we are going to explore some concrete strategies you can use, and teach your team to use, when one of these tough situations arises so that any challenge is only a small bump in the road and not a major detour.

We started with how you feel about challenging situations because it is important to recognize that we each have a natural response to difficult team dynamics. There are generally three ways to approach difficulties in a team: 1) avoid the situation, 2) confront the situation head-on, or 3) get curious about what is going on and try to problem-solve. In Chapter 2 we talked about the power of curiosity for coaches working one-on-one with colleagues. The same idea holds true when coaching teams. When there is something going on in a team, it is important to take some time to figure out what is going on and work with the team to resolve it.

Generally, when there is a difficult dynamic arising, there is a real issue that needs to be addressed in order for the team to move forward. Facilitators can help to head off major situations by noticing and acknowledging signs of tension when they first arise. Avoiding addressing situations either provides unspoken consent that the behavior is acceptable, or can lead to the behaviors getting worse over time. In either case, it is much harder to redirect the longer you wait. Conversely, confronting the situation head-on and trying to control or fix people within the team dynamic can also lead to poor team outcomes.

Instead, when difficult situations arise within the team, it is best to get curious about why the behaviors are occurring. Instead of getting frustrated, take a breath and remember that this person is doing the best they can with what they have right now. Put on your detective hat and try to figure out where the behavior is coming from or what it is symptomatic of. Many difficult dynamics arise when members of the team don't feel heard or supported. Use your judgment to decide whether the conversation is best had with individuals outside the team meeting or whether it is something that needs to be addressed during the meeting itself. When you exhibit compassionate curiosity for team members who are struggling, you have a chance to model this behavior. When your whole team can work from a place of compassionate curiosity to resolve conflict, solutions that work for everyone are developed and the team can move ahead again stronger for having weathered the storm.

In addition to maintaining our stance of curiosity, there are some moves we can make when we facilitate groups that are helpful to interrupt difficult situations when they first arise. A word of caution about these moves: like many coaching moves, the way you enact them is more important than how you say them. Tone and body language play a big role in how they are received. Every move on the list below can be positively received or the opposite. Make sure you are in a calm place before you try any of these moves to avoid them backfiring and escalating the situation further. With that caveat in mind, let's look at some intervention techniques originally developed by conflict resolution experts and drawn from a number of sources:

1. *Boomerang.* Send questions back to the team to be answered. For example, if a team member says, "Why are we talking about moving to this platform? Isn't the system we have fine?" The facilitator can respond, "Can the team remind us how we made the decision to move to this platform?" This move takes the focus off of the facilitator and returns ownership for the work to the team.
2. *Maintain or Regain Focus.* Note the discussion has lost its focus or moved away from the topic. The purpose of this move is to call attention to the fact that the team is off task. Generally, this simple move will either cause the team to get back on track or will raise a conversation about why the digression is necessary and then the team can move on from there. This might sound something like, "According to our agenda, we are supposed to be reviewing the data from last week's quiz in order to help us clarify our inquiry focus. However, we are currently discussing what happened at lunch. Can we return to our agenda item?"

Referring to the agenda as a common authority or "third point" can be a useful strategy that helps all team members remain on the same page. It does not pit one team member against another, but rather helps the team as a whole to return their focus to a previously agreed upon common focus.

3. *Ask a "Naive" Question.* Ask the team to explain a behavior to you. For example, "Where on the agenda are we right now?" or, "I'm confused. What is happening right now?" These types of questions require the team to check itself without you necessarily having to direct the course of the action.

4. *Say What Is Going On.* If you notice something going on, you can simply identify and describe the behavior. You might say something like, "I am noticing a number of team members are having side conversations. Is there something we need to discuss as a team?" This requires the team to also note the behavior and either correct it or explain it.

5. *Check for Agreement.* Never assume that the team agrees with your statements or suggestions. Ask them instead. This might sound like, "Do we all agree that our next agenda will include time for this topic?" This helps the team to own the decisions and the ripples caused by those decisions, not just the facilitator.

6. *Avoid Procedural Disputes.* Ask for group approval of process or changes to the process. For example, you might say, "We are out of time for this item on our agenda. Do we want to continue this discussion or move on?" Like checking for agreement, this move helps the team to own the direction of the discussion and how the work proceeds.

7. *Enforce Process Agreements.* Help the team uphold agreements they have made. You might say something like, "Starting on time is one of our team's norms. So, although we are currently missing two team members, we are going to start. They can join the discussion when they arrive." Helping the team adhere to norms and agreements helps the team to maintain trust in each other and belief in the processes you have worked so hard with the team to form.

8. *Encourage.* Notice and support team members and the team as a whole throughout the process. This could include noting when team members are not contributing, for example, "We haven't heard from Sandra yet today. What is your perspective on this?" or, it could mean encouraging the team as they work hard to understand one another and come to consensus. This could sound like, "I so appreciate how this team is willing to work through difficult issues

together and your belief that you will work through these issues with the support of each other."

9. *Legitimize.* Sharing ideas with the team can be a risky move for certain team members. Modeling respect for all ideas, therefore, is a powerful facilitation tool. For example, you could say, "I appreciate that you were willing to share a different perspective on this topic. It's so important that we consider all sides of this issue before deciding how to proceed." Because of your role in the team, your legitimation can help members to see more worth in the ideas of others as well.

10. *Use Criticism Appropriately.* We all make mistakes and, sometimes, facilitators take the brunt of the frustration of the team. Don't be defensive and apologize as appropriate. Calmly say something like, "Thank you for noting that we are ending late today which does not match with our norms. We will work to stay within our time at our next meeting." Your grace in these situations will diffuse the anger and be a model for others.

11. *Use Body Language Effectively.* It isn't always about what you say. Sometimes how you situate yourself in the room and in relation to the other members of the team speaks volumes. For example, you can sit down if things are going well, legitimize the ideas of others by nodding, or use hand gestures to halt interruptions.

12. *Use Group Memory.* Instead of debating with team members or rehashing previous discussions, it is helpful to ask the team to reference the agenda or notes from previous meetings to resolve the situation. You could say, "Let's go back to our notes from last week. How did we come to this agreement?" Like maintaining or regaining focus, referencing a third point such as notes from a previous meeting can help the team stay a team while moving forward.

In any given situation, a facilitator can respond in a variety of ways. How you choose to respond should take into consideration what you know about the people, the process, and the outcomes you are working to achieve. Different choices lead you, and the team, down different paths. For example, if a team member says, "It's time to make a decision. We've been discussing this for 20 minutes already." The facilitator could check for agreement with the team, and say "Do we all agree that we are ready to make a decision?" or, the facilitator could enforce process agreements and say, "I am glad you are feeling ready to make a decision. We agreed we would follow this protocol for making a decision. The protocol allots 25 minutes for discussion and then there will be time for determining next steps." Each of these choices has a different potential outcome for the team and its work together. It is up to the facilitator to make that call. The best question a facilitator can ask herself is, "What do I most want to have happen here?" Your answer to that question will help you to choose the right technique and ask the right question to keep your team positive, focused, and productive.

Utilizing these techniques can aid a facilitator—or any participant in the meeting—to help the team continue to work together in a positive manner, stay on task and on track to meet short- and long-term goals, and address and reduce challenges in a productive manner. Learning to use these techniques smoothy and appropriately in the moment takes time to master. There is no shame in having this list in front of you while you facilitate, especially at the beginning. Pick a few that sound like you and try them out, refine them, and make them your own. When those are working for you, pick a few more to add to your repertoire, and so on. Many masterful facilitators keep such notes as a reminder for themselves about their options and the possibilities that each situation provides to help the team.

At the end of each and every group coaching situation, there are a few key tasks that the facilitator must ensure are accomplished before the group disperses.

1. Take time to debrief the protocol or the meeting as a whole.
2. Make or review agreements about next steps with the group.
3. Make sure agreements are documented and share these with the group in written form.
4. Check in with anyone who presented to ensure they got what they needed and to get feedback on their experience.
5. Reflect on your own facilitation efforts. Don't be too hard on yourself!
6. Plan for next time.

Taking the time to complete these tasks before you walk away from a meeting will help you to ensure good ideas don't get lost between meetings. It is also a great opportunity for you to model for your teammates the importance of taking time to reflect and improve as a constant part of our work as educational professionals.

We Had a Good Meeting . . . Now What? Creating Long-Term Team Success

Congratulations on your successful team coaching session. Your agenda helped keep everyone on track, those norms were helpful, and the protocol helped

Figure 4.10 Creating Long-Term Team Success

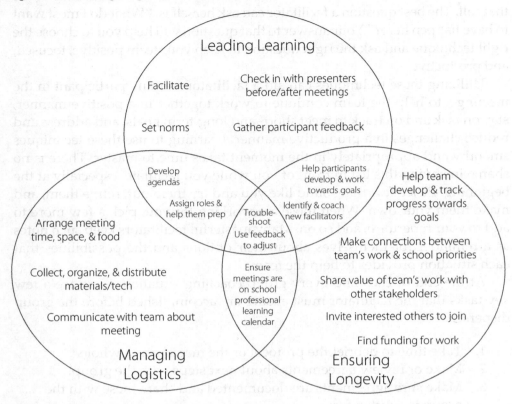

Leading Learning

Facilitate

Check in with presenters before/after meetings

Set norms

Gather participant feedback

Develop agendas

Help participants develop & work towards goals

Help team develop & track progress towards goals

Assign roles & help them prep

Troubleshoot

Identify & coach new facilitators

Arrange meeting time, space, & food

Use feedback to adjust

Make connections between team's work & school priorities

Collect, organize, & distribute materials/tech

Ensure meetings are on school professional learning calendar

Share value of team's work with other stakeholders

Communicate with team about meeting

Invite interested others to join

Find funding for work

Managing Logistics

Ensuring Longevity

Adapted from the work of Harvard's Project Zero

your team develop some keen new insights. Great job! If your team will meet more than once, you aren't done yet, however. The time you spend between meetings with your team is as important as the time you spend in those meetings because it is this in-between-time that helps to keep the momentum going and the work moving ahead.

Figure 4.10 is a useful graphic Emily developed based on the work of Harvard's Project Zero. She keeps this in her office as a regular reminder about the important work that happens between group coaching sessions.

As Figure 4.10 depicts, there are three categories of work for facilitators of teams: leading learning, managing logistics, and ensuring longevity. We've written a lot in this chapter about the items that fall under the leading learning section like skills for facilitation and norm setting. We think the logistics pieces are pretty straightforward as they are primarily managerial tasks. However, it is the items in the ensuring longevity circle that can make or break a team's work in schools. A coach is uniquely situated in a school to be able to see beyond the work of the team to other school priorities, and share about the work of the team with important stakeholders who will value what the team is doing and find ways to support the team in continuing successfully. Promoting the work of the team, or at least helping understand how the team's work contributes to larger organizational learning and goals is critical to ensuring funding is allocated to the work and not cut when budgets get tight (and they are always tight in schools).

Finally, in the overlapping space between leading learning and ensuring longevity, note the item that reads, "identify & coach new facilitators." One of the most important roles of a coach is to see the leadership potential in others and help them to grow that skill set. The best teams are the ones in which every member of the team is a leader, every member can facilitate, and every member is mindful of how to help the team move forward and skilled enough to help steer it in that direction. True leaders are not those who hold all the leadership for themselves, but seek to help others lead.

Look again at Figure 4.10 and consider which items on it are already strengths of yours as a coach and facilitator. Maybe put a plus next to them. Now consider which items are not yet strengths and could use your time and attention as you move forward in coaching groups. Perhaps put a delta or Δ next to them. Perhaps consider making a copy of this graphic and hanging it where you can see it as you plan for group coaching sessions so that you can ensure each of these items is addressed for your team.

Putting It All Together

In this chapter, we've unpacked the new skills that a coach needs to add to her repertoire when moving from coaching individuals to coaching teams and leading professional development. We considered the triangle of outcomes, people, process, and trust as a framework for coaching teams. We've delved into the research on the stages of team development and how they impact our work as team developers and facilitators. We've discussed proactive strategies such as norm setting, agenda development, and protocol usage for helping teams achieve their goals and work well together. We looked at moves we can make when things begin to go awry in a team meeting. And, finally, we looked at the three components of how to keep a team learning over time. In the next chapter, we will look at strategies coaches can use to gather data on the impact of their work on teaching and learning—a critical skill set for coaches who wish to improve their practice and show others the positive outcomes of coaching.

(continued)

(continued)

We'd like to leave you with two inspirational quotes to think about at the end of this chapter that, we hope, will resonate with you as you move into the rewarding and challenging arena of coaching groups: "You can't force commitment, what you can do . . . You nudge a little here, inspire a little there, and provide a role model. Your primary influence is the environment you create" (Peter Senge); "If you want to go fast, go alone. If you want to go far, go together" (African Proverb).

Note

1 One of our favorite websites for finding protocols is the School Reform Initiative (www.schoolreforminitiative.org/protocols/).

References

Kagan, L. (2007). *Dynamic Trainer*. San Clemente, CA: Kagan Publishing.

Leahy, D. (2004). *ATLAS: Looking At Data Protocol*. Retrieved from: www.schoolreforminitiative.org/protocols/.

Lencioni, P. (2002). *The Five Dysfunctions of a Team: A Leadership Fable*. San Francisco, CA: Jossey-Bass.

Senge, P.M. (1990). *The Fifth Discipline: The Art & Practice of the Learning Organization*. New York: Currency.

Thompson-Grove, G. (2000). *Consultancy Protocol*. Retrieved from: www.schoolreforminitiative.org/protocols/.

Tuckman, B.W. (1965). Developmental sequence in small groups. *Psychological Bulletin*, 63(6), 384–399.

5

How's It Going?
Gathering and Sharing Data on the
Impact of Coaching

For some people, data is an ugly four-letter word. Coaches often feel that the best use of their time is to coach, not to do research. However, we've seen too many cases in which great coaching programs and great coaches are cut in difficult budget years or when there is a change in leadership because the coach cannot prove that the work she is doing is making a difference. This is especially true for tech coaches who are often hired when a district has already spent copious amounts of money to purchase technologies and wants to be able to show their stakeholders that their investment was worthwhile. Therefore, creating and implementing a plan to determine the impact of coaching on teaching and learning is a critical skill for a tech coach to have.

There are so many kinds of data available to coaches and it is sometimes difficult to know what to look at and what to do with it. In this chapter, we will explore:

◆ a data collection and impact continuum;
◆ consider strategies for analyzing and utilizing the data to improve practice; and
◆ explore approaches to sharing this data with stakeholders in ways that will promote programmatic longevity and sustainability.

What Should We Collect?

First, let us be clear that there is no expectation that a novice tech coach or a new program leader will begin their work with a full-blown data collection, analysis, and communications plan. Effective data collection is carefully done over a long period of time and is often instituted incrementally. With that in mind, let's take a look at the kinds of data that one can collect, why you might collect it, and how you would go about doing so.

Generally, there are two types of data available to program leaders and tech coaches: data on the *implementation* of the program and data on the *impact* of the program. Implementation data is generally easier to access and more quickly available—it includes items you can count and artifacts you and your team might have created. Impact data, on the other hand, takes more time to access and longer to develop. It includes information about how the work is changing the climate, practice, and learning. Take a look at the continuum in Figure 5.1.

Let's take a look at each of these categories of data in turn and consider why you would collect such data and what might be collected.

Implementation Metrics

Generally, the first questions we have about a coaching program are how it is being enacted and how close to our vision of success it is adhering. Implementation data tells the story of how a program is being executed and focuses primarily on two areas—counting metrics and program quality metrics.

1. *Counting Metrics.* This is the easiest of all data to collect and is exactly what its name implies—things you can count. It is also a great place to start when beginning a data collection program because it can help to paint a picture in broad strokes about the reach of a program.

Figure 5.1 Coaching Impact Spectrum

Counting	Program Quality	Practice	Student Outcomes
Who are we reaching?	*How well is the program being implemented?*	*How and in what ways is practice becoming more effective?*	*How and in what ways are student outcomes improving?*
Implementation Metrics		**Impact Metrics**	

Adapted from New Teacher Center *Impact Spectrum* (2011)

Generally, counting metric questions begin with phrases such as "how many," "how much," or "how often." For example:

a. How many tech coaches do we have?
b. How many teachers are working with tech coaches?
c. How many sessions/hours are coaches working with teachers individually/in teams?
d. How many schools is each tech coach responsible for supporting?
e. How many teachers is each coach supporting at a given time?
f. How often are tech coaches working with individual teachers/teams of teachers?
g. How much are individual schools using tech coaches?

We can generally answer these types of questions as part of a coaching accountability program (if we are program leaders) or through record keeping of our own work (if we are tech coaches). For example, many programs ask coaches to keep a basic log of some sort like the one we offered in Chapter 1 (Figure 1.4) and below in Figure 5.2.

A tech coach or program leader could easily use these logs over time to determine the number of teachers a coach is seeing each week or over time and how often the coach is visiting with each teacher. It would be easy to quickly build a table for stakeholders that shows the reach of the program, to notice trends in the data, and to even begin to make adjustments to coach allocation or to determine which schools might need more support. While counting metrics can only give a 30,000-foot view of a coaching program's work, it is an incredibly useful place to start.

2. *Program Quality Metrics.* As its name implies, this type of data strives to capture an understanding of the level of fidelity a program has to its quality goals. Instead of asking how many/how much questions, program quality metrics ask more "what" and "how well" questions. For example:

Figure 5.2 Coaching Log Example

Teacher	Date/Time	Topics	Tasks
Ms. G	2/2/18, 3rd period	Ongoing formative Assessment	Using Google Forms to drive real-time feedback
Mr. C	2/3/18, 5th period	Student Voice	Integrating Flipgrid and Qball to promote student's voice

a. How are coaches and teachers/teams spending their time together? (i.e. What coaching processes are they using? What artifacts are they creating?)

b. What types of technology applications are coaches helping to implement to enhance learning experiences?

c. How well are coaches being received by teachers/teams/schools?

For program leaders, this is incredibly important data. It fills in the broad strokes of the picture developed from looking at counting metrics to give a broader understanding of the quality of the work that is occurring. It can help the program leader know, for example, if coaches are using coaching language and/or tools that have been shared in coaching professional development sessions and how well they are using them. It can also help the program leader to know where things are not going as well and intervene or adjust to improve the quality of support teachers are getting. For individual coaches, looking at their own data can also help to uncover trends in time usage, areas of interest or need in their coaching clients, and use feedback from clients to adjust practice.

There are a number of ways that a coach or program leader could gather program quality data.

For example, a program leader, or two coaches working together, could engage in an in-field coaching cycle with a coach in which they pre-conference to talk about what the coach and client are working on together and what the coach is trying to do, observe coaching happening in the field, and then debrief the session together. The template below (Figure 5.3) might be useful for organizing an in-field coaching cycle like we've described here.

Coaches or programs can also ask coaching clients to provide anonymous feedback on a regular basis that can be disaggregated and used to consider strengths and necessary adjustments in the coaching program. Figure 5.4 (below) is an example of a quick survey that could help a coach or program leader get a sense of how teachers working with coaches are perceiving the work:

In an ideal case, program leaders and coaches are triangulating across a number of these data sources to get a clearer sense about program quality. While these types of data sources take more time to gather and analyze, they also create a much clearer understanding of how the program is being enacted and the quality with which is it being implemented. At the end of this chapter, we have included some templates you might use or adapt to gather some of this data for yourselves.

Figure 5.3 In-Field Coach Observation Protocol

In-Field Coach Observation Protocol

Pre-Observation Conference

1. Who are you going to be coaching in this session? What are you working on together?
2. What are your coaching goals for this session? (i.e. What coaching moves are you planning to try? What outcomes are you aiming for?)
3. What kind of data can I gather for you that would help you know if you are meeting your goals?
4. Logistics: when, where, time of observation? Post-observation?
5. How will technology be integrated to address the needs of learners?

Observation
Gather factual data (not opinion) focused on the area agreed upon in the pre-observation conference. The goal is to share this data with the coach in the post-observation session.

An option for collecting data is to create a chart like this:

Time	Coach Words/ Actions	Teacher Words/Actions	Observer Questions/ Wonderings

Another option, if observing in classrooms, might look like this:

Time	What is the Teacher Doing with Tech?	What are Students Doing with Tech?	Observer Questions/ Wonderings

A third option, if observing in classrooms, might look like this:

Time	How is technology providing students with choice in how they show what they know about the topic at hand?	How is the technology amplifying student voice?	Observer Questions/ Wonderings

Post-Observation Conference

1. Remind the teacher about his/her goal. How close to your goal do you feel you got? How/why?
2. Review data gathered during observation.
   a. What helped you to get to your goal?
   b. Where were there missed opportunities?
3. What are your next steps based on this data?
4. What supports might you need to help take these next steps?
5. How has engaging in this coaching observation impacted you?
6. What might I do better next time?
7. Did the planned technology integration meet your objectives?

Figure 5.4 Anonymous Coaching Client Survey Example

Anonymous Coaching Client Survey Example

Our program strives to provide useful and meaningful coaching support. We need your help to make sure we are doing so! Please consider your work with a technology coach over the last semester and respond to the questions below:

1. I generally work with the technology coach
   a. One-on-one exclusively
   b. As part of a team exclusively
   c. Both one-on-one and as part of a team
   d. I have not worked with a technology coach

2. On average, I work with a technology coach
   a. Daily
   b. Weekly
   c. Monthly
   d. Every once in a while
   e. Not at all

3. On average, each session with the technology coach has lasted
   a. More than an hour
   b. 30 minutes-1 hour
   c. Less than 30 minutes

4. As a result of working with a technology coach, I have felt more confident in working with technology.
   a. Very true
   b. Somewhat true
   c. No change

5. As a result of working with a technology coach, I have implemented a new technology in my classroom.
   a. Yes
   b. No

6. Which elements of the SAMR model were addressed when adding technology to the lesson or unit of study in which you worked with the tech coach?
   a. Substitution
   b. Augmentation
   c. Modification
   d. Redefinition

7. Overall, I have had a positive experience working with the technology coach.
   a. Strongly agree
   b. Somewhat agree
   c. Somewhat disagree
   d. Strongly disagree

8. What has worked for you about working with the technology coach?
9. What changes/improvements could the technology coach or the coaching program make that would improve your experience?

Thank you for your feedback!

For stakeholders, implementation data helps tell the story of what is actually happening with real people and how they are receiving the supports offered by the program. We can tell you from experience that stakeholders are generally more hesitant to cut programs that can show how many people are taking advantage of a program and how much people appreciate the program. If you are able to create a plan that helps you to gather these two types of data in the first year of your program, you will be far ahead of most other initiatives and will have plenty of data to support you in refining and honing your program as well as telling the story of your program to interested others.

Impact Metrics

Knowing that your coaching or coaching program is making a difference is critical to your success. In order to measure this, you will need to do a deeper dive into metrics that will help you understand what, if any, change in practice and in student learning is occuring as a result of your work.

1. *Practice Metrics.* The theory behind implementing coaching programs of any kind is that teaching and learning will improve more rapidly with support from a coach than it would without that intervention. To determine if that theory is correct, we would ask questions such as:

   a. How, if at all, are teachers improving as a result of coaching? How do we know?
   b. Under what circumstances do teachers seem more or less ready to implement new technology with coaching supports?
   c. How does the tech use of teachers receiving coaching supports compare to those not receiving such supports?
   d. How are teachers leveraging the power of professional learning communities and personal learning networks in the physical and virtual worlds to learn more about what is and is not impactful when implementing instructional technologies?

   If the implementation metrics helped point us in a general direction of what is successful or not with a coaching program or practice, these metrics help provide a deeper, richer, and more qualitative sense of why and how a program is making a difference (or not).

   Gauging the impact you or your tech coaching program is having on teacher practice is trickier because there are often many factors, in addition to your work with the teacher, which might influence their speed of uptake and quality of tech integration into their practice. These factors might include: their current level of will and skill around teaching generally (see Chapter 2 for more on will and skill); the current climate in the school or team and the riskiness of trying new things in that climate; the number of initiatives teachers are currently being asked to tackle; or their feelings about, or experiences with, technology both in and outside of education. While measuring coaching impact on change in teaching practice can be tricky, it is still critical that we begin to gather data from a number of sources that, collectively, can give us a better sense of what is making a difference and under what circumstances we are more or less successful.

So, how do we gather this kind of data? While there is a large range of potential artifacts or processes we can take to get a sense of programmatic impact, the clearest and most compelling way is to triangulate across a number of sources. Take a look at the Figure 5.5 below for one example.

In this example, the coach/coaching program looks to three sources for information: the coach, the teacher, and the principal. Each of these stakeholders in the coaching process can provide different perspectives and artifacts that provide a piece of understanding. For example, in-field observations of the coach working with a teacher can provide insight into moves the coach is making that seem to lead to higher levels of uptake by teachers. We could couple that with a review of the lesson plan the teacher created that integrates the technology she discussed with the coach to see the teacher's conceptual understanding of how to best use the technology in her class. For even stronger data, we could watch

Figure 5.5 Data Triangulation for Practice Impact

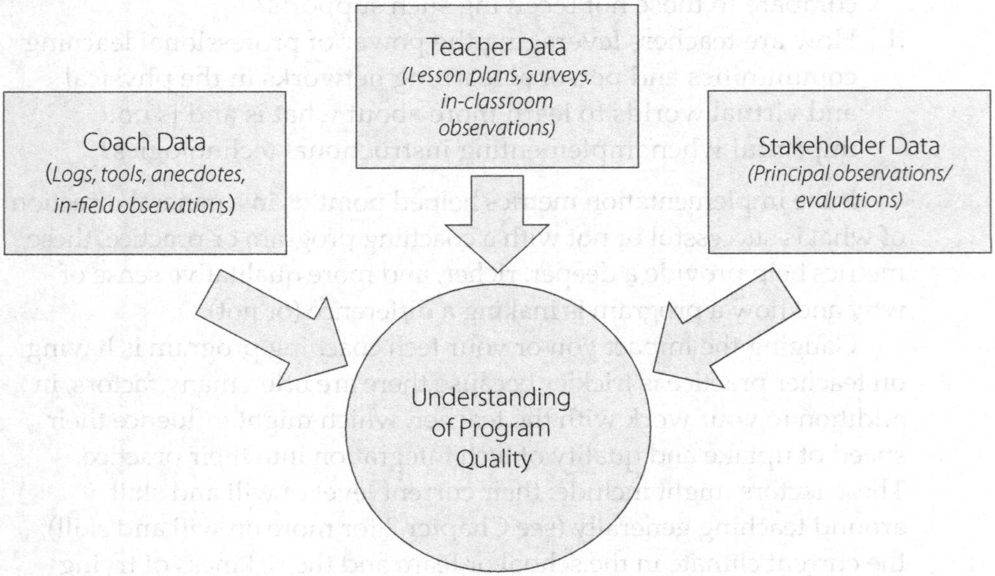

Coach Data
(*Logs, tools, anecdotes, in-field observations*)

Teacher Data
(*Lesson plans, surveys, in-classroom observations*)

Stakeholder Data
(*Principal observations/ evaluations*)

Understanding of Program Quality

the teacher teach the lesson and see if the implementation matched the lesson and if it was successful. We could then speak with the principal about what she is seeing in the teacher's classroom and if she has a similar sense of the teacher's success.

Each of these perspectives brings a new level of depth and clarity to the understanding of how the work between the coach and the teacher is directly impacting the practice of the teacher. Coaches can do this kind of work on their own, with others, or as a team to really understand what they are doing or might do that can improve both their practice and teacher practice. In and of itself, this kind of program quality review is phenomenal professional learning for any coach or coaching program to undertake. Furthermore, being able to tell this kind of story using data such as the ones described here as corroboration is compelling evidence to any stakeholder group that you take this work seriously, seek to understand and improve outcomes, and are deserving of continued funding and support.

2. *Student Outcome Metrics.* Understanding how coaching is impacting student outcomes is, by far, the most difficult to unpack. While there are numerous factors that can impact a teacher's ability to grow with coach support, there are even more variables between coach input and student output that can confound our understanding of coaching on student outcomes. For this reason, some researchers refer to student learning metrics as "the holy grail of coaching research." While student impact data is challenging to gather, it should not stop coaches or program leaders from making efforts to gather data indicating a correlation between coaching and student outcomes. To drive this kind of research, we can ask questions such as:

   a. In what ways are teachers implementing technology in their classrooms that seem to have a positive influence on student outcomes?
   b. How, if at all, are student outcomes improving as a result of changes in teacher practice connected to coaching?
   c. How has technology, coupled with pedagogically-sound teaching methods, impacted student outcomes?
   d. Are certain students more/less successful as a result of the change in practice?
   e. How does the tech use of students in classrooms where teachers are receiving coaching supports compare to those in classrooms not receiving such supports?
   f. How do student outcomes in classrooms where teachers are receiving coaching supports compare to those in classrooms not receiving such supports?

Basically, we are making the hypothesis that if students are in classrooms where teachers are implementing technology well, their outcomes will improve. Then the research work is to answer questions such as those listed above in order to make a strong link between coaching inputs and student outcomes with a bridge of data between them.

Note that we are using the term student *outcomes* instead of student *learning* here on purpose. We believe that the term student outcomes represents a whole-child approach whereas student learning focuses educators too narrowly on only academic achievement. When coaches support teachers in implementing technology, there is a range of positive outcomes that can occur. For example, consider a school that uses blended learning in which content is taught using an online system and then students work in small groups to practice utilizing content along with collaborative skills. Teachers in this school have reported that students with special needs are much more successful because it is not evident to them or to other students that they have different learning needs. The result being that students do not give up as easily, nor do other students assume that these students are not able to be full partners in group activities. This has led to both improved academic and social outcomes for students with special needs in this school. As you think about gathering student outcome data, we encourage you to consider ways in which technology integration in teaching practice might positively benefit the whole range of student experiences.

Figure 5.6 Data Triangulation for Student Outcomes Impact

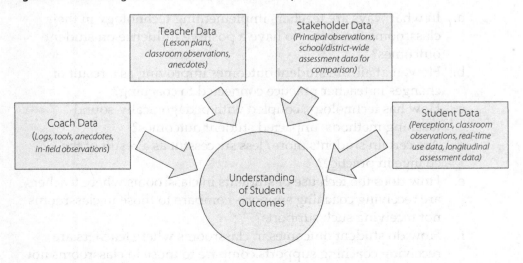

Like gathering teacher practice data, student outcomes data also requires triangulation from multiple stakeholders across multiple sources. Figure 5.6 contains one example of what this might look like in practice:

Student outcomes metrics may require us to gather data from a wider range of stakeholders. In this example, we could again observe coaching practice for moves that seem to lead to greater uptake of thoughtful instructional technology use in the teacher's practice and look at how and when the students are using technology in the classroom. We could then look at the assessment data for this class and compare it to other grade-level, school, or district-wide assessment data to notice any differences. If, for example, we could say with some degree of correlational certainty, that a strategy for using a new technology introduced by the coach, and implemented well by the teacher, led to student achievement gains that were significantly higher than those of other teachers in the same grade-level, we can say with reasonable certainty that coaching had an impact on student outcomes. Understanding this chain of causality from you as the coach through the teacher to students is an important process for you to understand. Being able to unpack what moves you made that led the teacher to successfully implement something that, in turn, impacted a student can help you improve your practice. Learning how others in your coaching program are making deliberate moves that lead to positive outcomes can also be deeply transformative for your coaching practice. Further, since most programs and coaches do not do the work to make this kind of important connection, if you are able to show that kind of evidence to stakeholders with data to back up your claims, they will shake your hand and do a little dance of happiness . . . and you will definitely get to keep your job.

Having a plan from the beginning to gather data is crucial. It is also easy to get lost in the data. There are so many types of data you could collect and analyze, but not all of them are worth your time at this moment. Our suggestion is to get really clear about what your goals are as a program and individually (See Chapter 6 for more on goal setting) and then create a data collection plan that will help you, and your stakeholders, know if you are meeting those goals. Start small and doable with your plan and then build on over time. Doing so will ensure you can actually stick to your plan and have data that will support growth and sustainability for you and/or your program.

What Do We Do with What We Have Collected?

Whether you or your program are at the beginning stages of data collection or have a more sophisticated process for gathering data in place, it is important to have a plan for how you will use that data. As we have alluded to in the previous section, data that you have collected and analyzed is useful to you as a coach or as a program leader in two ways:

1. personal or internal program use for continuous improvement; and
2. external sharing with stakeholders to show accountability to program goals and other outcomes valued by the larger decision-making community.

While the ultimate goal in the data collection and analysis process should be to ensure coaching is making positive progress towards programmatic, school, and/or district goals, the way this data is used and shared will differ when meant for internal versus external use. Let's take a look at each in turn.

1. *Personal or Internal Program Use for Continuous Improvement.* The clearest goal of data collection and analysis for most tech coaches and program leaders is to truly understand what is working and what is not working in a coaching practice and why. From a programmatic perspective, gathering and sharing data with your team, taking the time to review it, discuss its implications, celebrate successes, and brainstorm strategies for improvement can be phenomenal professional development. It promotes buy-in, helps to develop common vision, and leads to articulation and refinement of best practices. If you are a coach working on your own, consider making time each week or each month to review your data in a systematic way and to make strategic decisions about what you should keep doing or change. Find others who you trust with whom you can share your data and brainstorm ideas.

   So how do we actually look at all this data? Although there are many different data protocols that can help, a few simple questions (or, a protocol, if you will) can empower coaches to reflect upon almost any data source. Here are a set of questions Emily developed with fellow coach, Kenny McKee, for a 2015 blog post entitled "Making Data Your Superpower":

   1. What is the data measuring?
   2. What *observations* can we make about the data?
   3. What *inferences* can we make about the data?

4. In which areas do we have influence or control?
5. What actions can we take now based upon our analysis of the data?

Whether looking at one data source or many, these questions can help you and/or your team to orient themselves in a productive way to the data, see what is actually present, and understand how to move forward realistically.

Whether you are on your own or part of a program, consider how using technology can support you in organizing your collected data for easy review and analysis. For example, if you or your team is using a log to gather information about coaching meetings, you could turn that log into a Google Form. The Form populates a Google Sheet that can help you see and manipulate all of your data and/or your team's data quickly and efficiently. A table that looks like the one below (Figure 5.7) is much easier to review quickly than sifting through paper logs, for example.

A team reviewing this data might quickly note, for example, that coaches 1 and 2 are doing a lot more group coaching, but coach 3 is doing a lot more one-one-one coaching. Why? Coaches 2 and 3, on the other hand, are spending a lot more time observing in classrooms than coach 1. Why? This type of data often leads to more questions. The questions are what lead to improvement.

For a coach working on her own, using a Google Form log is also helpful. Take a look at the example in Figure 5.8.

Again, the reviewer of this data could quickly note that while all three of these teachers attended the team coaching session, the most time is being spent with teacher 3 while teacher 2 is not utilizing coaching outside the group at all this month. Why? Getting curious about your own data and seeking to understand the story behind it, what it means for your coaching, and how you can use it over time to improve is incredibly powerful.

However you go about sharing and analyzing your data, make sure that you are making regular time and space to do so. The process

Figure 5.7 Monthly Coaching Time Report Google Sheet Example 1

Coach	One-on-One Coaching (Hours)	Team Coaching (Hours)	Classroom Observation (Hours)	Total Interactions	Average Interaction Length (Hours)
1	63.5	33	6	100	1.03
2	78	20	22	62	1.94
3	130	2	18	117	1.28

Figure 5.8 Monthly Coaching Time Report Google Sheet Example 2

Teacher	One-on-One Coaching (Hours)	Team Coaching (Hours)	Classroom Observation (Hours)	Total Interactions
1	4	1	1	5
2	0	1	0	1
3	12	1	2	10

of data review and analysis does not have to be a lengthy one. In fact, you are far more likely to look at data regularly and do something useful with it if you have a quick and efficient protocol for doing so. It is not useful if data analysis is only done after the semester or year is over. Real-time analysis and adjustment—that cycle of continuous improvement—is what helps programs and coaches to improve at a rapid rate. As we've mentioned before, take the data review process as a chance to get curious, play detective, and truly seek to understand what's going on. It's easy to only search for data that confirms what you want to see and ignore anything that doesn't fit that pattern. Use your coaching detective skills to seek patterns, look for disconfirming evidence, and find out what is going on and why.

2. *External Sharing with Stakeholders.* Many coaches and program leaders have commented to us that, when they first began, they didn't understand the value of sharing data with stakeholders beyond their current group. They thought that if they did their jobs well that everything would be fine. Or, as many educators do, they felt that sharing with stakeholders about their programs felt like self-promotion or bragging and they weren't comfortable with that concept. Our first hurdle as tech coaches or program leaders is to reframe why we must share about what we do. When we do not share what we are doing and how it is working with those who make the decisions about how to allocate resources, we lose the opportunity to show how what we are doing adds value and helps to meet broader school or district goals. When we cannot show our worth, it is hard for others to justify continuing to resource our programs.

The goal of sharing with stakeholders must be to tell the story of what you are doing and how it is impacting others in a way that will speak best to your audience. For example, if you are planning to share data with the principal of your school or your dean, you need to think about what is most important from their perspective and then pull data accordingly to share with them. Most stakeholders will not have the time to look at the copious amounts of data you may have collected and analyzed internally, so you need to think about what is most important for them to know. What is working?

Why? What is challenging? Why? There is no need to shy away from talking about challenges. Data is often a great place to start conversations about resources you might need or supports they can offer, or changes that can be made structurally that will help you

Figure 5.9 Infographic Example

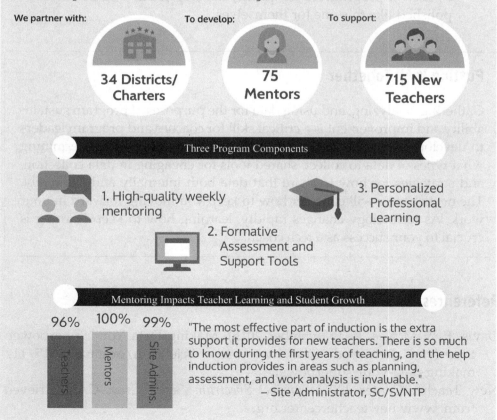

Reproduced with permission from the Santa Cruz/Silicon Valley New Teacher Project

all get to your common goal—a successful coaching program that is helping teachers and students succeed with technology.

With technology at our disposal, there are a myriad of ways that we can go about sharing our data with stakeholders. One of Emily's favorites is the use of *infographics*. These clean and clear displays can very quickly get the story of your data to your audience in an inviting and easily accessible manner. Take a look at this example from an organization Emily used to lead (Figure 5.9).

Very quickly, readers can get a sense of what this program does. One can see the scope of the work (counting metrics), the main components of the program (program implementation metrics), and participant response data (impact metrics). This program has posted this infographic on their website and shares it at meetings, conferences, and other venues to help others get a sense of who they are and what they do. It is a strong introductory data set that stakeholders and others can access and understand quickly. There are lots of free infographic makers available online that can help a coach or program leader quickly develop something clean and polished like this one for themselves.

Putting It All Together

Gathering, analyzing, and using data for the purposes of program sustainability and improvement is a critical skill for coaches and program leaders to develop. In this chapter we've looked at frameworks for determining what types of data to collect, shared tools for engaging in data collection, and strategies for how to share that data both internally and externally. The next chapter will consider how to keep you moving forward in your work. As technology changes rapidly, learning how to keep learning is crucial to your success as a tech coach.

References

Davis, E. & McKee, K. (November 2015). Making Data Your Superpower. *Smartbrief*. Retrieved from: www.smartbrief.com/original/2015/11/making-data-your-superpower.

New Teacher Center. (2011). *Impact Spectrum*. Santa Cruz, CA. Retrieved from: www.newteachercenter.org.

6

Staying Ahead of the Curve

Picture it, a small school district in Chester, New Jersey, decided to provide its staff with the opportunity of a lifetime—study for and take the Level I Google Certified Educator exam. The district believed that having this kind of training and knowledge would help the staff to stay ahead of the technology curve and be able to provide a 21st-century learning experience for all students. Would you believe that over 30 staff members took the district up on the offer and passed? Five of those 30 staff members took it a step further and earned the status of Google Certified Trainer. Pretty amazing right? School districts have amazing and talented staff, so why not let them reach for the stars and continue to enhance their effectiveness? None of these achievements in Chester would have been possible if it weren't for the support of the tech coaches. The coaches made sure they were knowledgeable and had a plan of support. For days, weeks, and months at a time, they provided tutorial sessions before, during, and after school. They made themselves available to their colleagues and exhausted all options to find answers to questions pertaining to the exam. That is why approximately one-fourth of the staff now have the unique distinction of being Level I Google Certified Educators.

Fortunately, there are stories like the one shared above taking place in districts all around the world. Unfortunately, there are still districts out there that do not support these sort of initiatives. The bottom line is that the Chester School District, in consultation with administration and the technology coaches, set a goal of providing staff with the opportunity to become Google Certified, implemented a plan to meet it, and marshaled resources to ensure its success. There are many risks involved with these kinds of initiatives and many things could have gone wrong: What if no one was interested in becoming Google Certified? What if more people failed than passed? Would the district be criticized for setting such an unattainable goal? In this case, the entire experience was a success. So how can tech coaches keep learning and staying ahead of the curve so they are ready to help others reach their goals?

This chapter will focus on how coaches can stay ahead of the curve by:

◆ setting professional goals using tech coaching standards and creating action plans to achieve them;
◆ evolving as educators;
◆ considering strategies and resources for continued learning;
◆ being lead learners; and
◆ reflecting on progress towards goals.

We hope you will walk away with a plan that will truly help you stay ahead of the curve and contribute to your school or district's future-ready environment.

Setting Professional Goals Using Tech Coaching Standards

Having a clear vision of the end state we are trying to achieve before we take action to reach our goals is the key factor in accomplishing any goals that we set. As tech coaches, we have to be conscious of goals at a variety of levels: the goals of the organization in which we work (i.e. our school, district, or university), the goals of the department or program in which we work (i.e. the coaching program or department), and our own professional goals as tech coaches or leaders. Our hope is that the goals set at each of these levels work in alignment with one another. It's important to note that we all have differing levels of control going into the goal- setting process. If you are a program leader, you may have control over the goals that are developed for your program and for yourself. If you are a coach, you may only have control over your own professional goals. Understanding what is within your sphere of influence and what is not, is a critical first step in setting realistic and attainable goals that will help propel you and those you support forward.

Regardless of the level of oversight you have in the goal-setting process, there are some common characteristics of effective goal-setting processes that are helpful to understand. By setting focused and clearly defined goals, you can plan a series of steps to help you achieve your goal and measure your progress towards those goals (see Chapter 5 for more on gathering data). Sharp and focused goals will also help you motivate yourself to progress towards the vision you have and increase your own confidence in your work.

The following are some general tips for setting effective goals:

- ◆ *Consider standards.* Seek out professional standards that can help you deepen your understanding of what your role requires. Use these standards as a jumping-off point for considering what areas for focus or growth might make good professional goals for you and/or your program.
- ◆ *Be positive.* Consider what you want to happen versus what you don't want and write your goals with that frame in mind.
- ◆ *Be realistic.* Setting a small goal that you can accomplish in a reasonable amount of time will ensure that you can achieve it and help keep your motivated.
- ◆ *Be specific.* The more precise you are about what success will look like and by when you will achieve the goal, the more likely you are to achieve it.
- ◆ *Prioritize.* Success tends to come when you know on which of your goals to focus your attention. Carefully select doable goals, get them done, and then set new ones.
- ◆ *Get small.* Break each goal down into a set of achievable steps, each with its own time frame for completion. This ensures you get frequent opportunities to celebrate accomplishments and will stay motivated to take on the next step towards your goal.

Figure 6.1 Tech Coach Goal Planner

Understanding the Larger Context	
District/school goals/areas of focus connected to my coaching work:	Program goals:
Understanding My Context	
Data from coaching clients or others that can help me determine areas of focus:	Relevant professional standard language connected to my area of focus:
Goal 1	
Positively framed goal (*Is it positive? Specific? Doable? Measurable? Most important?*):	Envision success (*What would it look like/sound like if you achieved your goal?*) Measuring success (*What data could you collect that would help you know if you are achieving this goal?*):
Action steps to achieve the goal (*Include specific actions, outcomes, and time frames for each step*):	Reflections on goal (*After completing the goal, reflect on what specific actions/steps you made that helped you achieve your goal. Could any of these be replicated next time? Also, consider what was challenging as you worked towards your goal. What might you improve next time?*):

◆ *Write it down*. Writing is thinking and, therefore, writing down goals helps us become more precise and clear. Written goals also serve as a visual reminder, so make sure to post your goals somewhere you will see them and refer to them regularly.

Figure 6.1 offers a template that might be useful for you to use or adapt when setting goals for yourself, or with your team, that encompasses the elements described above.

Let's take a look at some resources that can help you and/or your program set and achieve your professional tech coaching goals.

Professional Standards

It's important to know that there are organizations out there that have made available specific standards for instructional coaches. Two in particular, Future Ready Instructional Coaches and the ISTE Standards for Coaching[1] have helped highlight what truly is important when supporting educators in the digital world. Let's take a look at these two sets of standards and consider how they might be useful in the development of your professional goals and action plans.

1. Future Ready Instructional Coaches Framework

    Future Ready Schools coaches strengthen teacher instructional capacity by designing and modeling sound pedagogical practices. They create innovative, learner-driven experiences that meet teachers where they are and support them through their personalized learning pathway. In addition, instructional coaches advocate for infrastructure that ensures equitable access to connectivity, digital devices, information, resources, programming, and services for all students in support of the district's strategic vision.

    (https://futureready.org/program-overview/coaches/)

    The Future Ready Instructional Coaches Framework provides a look at the various areas of education that coaches impact on a consistent basis. From curriculum to infrastructure, instructional coaches play a pivotal role in ensuring that the needs of students are met in a pedagogically sound and innovative way. The section on budgets and resources is one we suggest you review as an instructional coach who leverages the power of technology. It's critical that coaches plan for the next school year well in advance so that programming is not altered in a negative way. If you were to set a goal focused on budgeting for technology, here are a set of action steps you might take to achieve your goal that are derived from this particular standard:

◆ Survey staff to see what types of different technologies and web applications they want to continue to use for the upcoming school year. Additionally, have them think about new "tools of the trade" they might want to pilot.

◆ Create a spreadsheet that contains a list of the technologies and various online platforms that teachers are interested in purchasing. Share the spreadsheet with the Director of Technology to make sure everything is compatible with the district's tech plan and infrastructure.

◆ Submit your wish list to the powers that be for final budgetary approval.

These small steps, collectively, would provide you and your program with data that would allow you to make a compelling case for how to use your limited financial resources while also helping your teachers and program to meet their goals.

2. ISTE Standards for Coaching

Technology coaches help bridge the gap from where we are to where we need to be. The ISTE Standards for coaching describe the skills and knowledge they need to support their peers in becoming digital age educators.

(www.iste.org/standards/for-coaches)

This set of standards clearly focuses on the ways in which technology coaches can improve the quality of instruction by supporting their peers. Let's take a look at one standard from this set and consider how it might be used to set a programmatic or coaching goal. ISTE Standard 5 focuses on Digital Citizenship. This is often a technology area of focus for districts or schools and, therefore, an area in which technology programs and coaches may need to set goals for themselves as well. According to the standard, when supporting teachers in helping students become responsible digital citizens, tech coaches need to consider the following questions when co-planning learning experiences:

◆ Is the online learning platform safe and protects student data and work?

◆ Do students understand their district's acceptable use policy and how to interact with others appropriately online?

◆ How is the assignment focused in on amplifying student voice in a positive way and impacting change for the greater good?

A coach could easily set a professional goal for herself that focuses on ISTE Standard 5 broadly or on any one of these sub-questions. She could create an action plan that would help her learn more about this important area, explore resources such as www.commonsense.org

(a site that provides information on websites and apps for educators that best suits the needs of students in various subject areas and learning abilities), and create a strategy for implementing a digital citizenship plan in the classrooms of the teachers she supports.

The ISTE standards are useful at all levels of PK-12 education to guide educators in integrating tech. Krista Welz is a School Librarian in North Bergen High School, New Jersey, and also teaches at New Jersey City University. Read on to learn how she uses these standards in her context (personal email):

> School librarians should be up-to-date on the latest research and educational technology trends in order to demonstrate confidence and proficiency when discussing and/or providing technological professional development to colleagues.
>
> One of my favorite courses to teach at New Jersey City University is a seminar course that is designed to explore the latest trends and research in curriculum and technology integration and explore how these trends affect instructional settings. The course's main objective is to have students provide evidence of their knowledge and expertise through the creation of a digital portfolio. Each page of their digital portfolio correlates to the 6 standards of ISTE Standards for Coaches. ISTE developed these standards to provide a framework for technology leaders to use as they transition schools from Industrial Age to Digital Age places of learning. By creating a digital portfolio with reflections of each standard and examples of work that the students have created to demonstrate their proficiency with the standard, students can demonstrate their skills as an effective technology leader.

As you can see, both resources highlight the important work that coaches do in the edtech world. Not only can these resources benefit coaches in reaching their goals, but also assist educators in understanding the connections technology and teaching have with one another. Through the positive connections that coaches make with their colleagues coupled with the infusion of pedagogically sound resources, learning environments can move from good to great in no time.

Evolve As an Educator

ISTE Standard 6 for Coaching speaks to the importance of content knowledge and professional growth for instructional coaches, but building an

Figure 6.2 Evolve as an Educator

E   **_Engage_** _in intentional professional growth opportunities that enhance your impact as an educator and promotes the success of all students._

V   **_Value_** _relationships, networking, and new opportunities to learn, teach, and lead in the physical and virtual worlds._

O   **_Orient_** _yourself to best practices that are innovative and push the limits of learning, teaching and leading._

L   **_Launch_** _yourself into new learning opportunities that promote professional risk-taking and educational autonomy._

V   **_Validate_** _your new knowledge and skills by demonstrating cutting edge tools and methods that empower learning, teaching, and leading._

E   **_Embody_** _the characteristics of an evolved educator as you learn, teach, lead, and advocate for others to evolve._

www.evolvingeducators.com
© Evolving Educators LLC

action plan to achieve a professional goal as a coach can be a daunting task. Where do you start? What steps should you take? What should the journey look like? Evolving Educators has designed a framework called EVOLVE that can support you on your journey towards your goal. Here are the tenets of the EVOLVE construct (Figure 6.2).

So, what does the EVOLVE framework look like in practice? Let's take each tenet in turn:

1. It's really important for coaches to **engage** in intentional professional learning opportunities. For example, Twitter has taken the educational world by storm over the past several years. In Brad's book that he co-wrote in 2016 with Billy Krakower and Scott Rocco, *140 Twitter Tips for Educators*, it's made very clear the type of positive pathway educators can make for themselves in 140 (now 280) characters or less. Attending innovative educational conferences, such as the annual Tomorrow's Classrooms Today Conference, will expose instructional coaches to pedagogically sound methods that challenge traditional learning spaces. It all comes down to networking in virtual or physical environments. Ideas and resources shared during these types of experiences ultimately impact the success of students.

2. Once engaged in relevant professional learning experiences, coaches should then **value** their educational belief system by surrounding themselves with other forward-thinking educators in the physical and virtual worlds. It will pay off in the long run if they are truly looking to evolve as an educator and impact the effectiveness of colleagues. Edcamps (www.edcamp.org/), for example, provide educators with an opportunity to learn in an informal setting. Participants have the freedom to hold conversations and choose the types of sessions they want to attend. Recently educators have taken to tools like Flipgrid and Instagram to connect and learn from others. Both "tools of the trade" give users an opportunity to hear and see others as they share their insight on a variety of educational topics. Make it a goal over the coming months to attend a local Edcamp and/or utilize a new tool like Flipgrid or Instagram to stay fresh with what's current.

3. Once engaged and validated coaches must then **orient** themselves with innovative best practices that push the limits of learning environments. There is no better way to gain exposure to best practices than by leveraging the power of Professional Learning Networks or PLNs. This could mean different things to different folks, but the bottom line is that instructional coaches must take advantage of these networks. For example, educators from around the country tune into Twitter each Saturday morning from 7:30–8:30 EST for #Satchat to discuss topics ranging from educational technology to digital citizenship to student voice. The more coaches orient themselves to best practices in the field of education utilizing digital tools, the better chance teacher effectiveness and student success will be impacted.

4. As much as possible, coaches must **launch** themselves into unchartered territories that promote risk-taking and autonomy. The more tech coaches model risk-taking, the more teachers will take risks.

The more teachers model taking risks, the more students take risks. Evolving as an educator takes time and, undoubtedly, failures will occur every so often. It's important to remember that this is a natural part of the learning process. Setbacks should not deter you from continuing to exploring new methods and tools. Your attitude about innovation will positively impact school culture and norms and will ultimately translate into teachers and students experiencing the same sort of freedom. There is no doubt that risk-taking and autonomous learning environments breed innovation and higher levels of learning.

5.   Above all else, it's critical that coaches **validate** their new knowledge and skills by demonstrating cutting edge tools and methods that empower learning, teaching, and leadership in the physical and virtual worlds. Additionally, technology coaches must empower those that they support by validating the great work they have done as a teacher. Some options include writing a blog post, presenting at a faculty meeting, or inviting a colleague into the classroom to observe part of a lesson.Finally, **embody** what a current and evolving educator truly is. What does this look like? It's everything described above within the EVOLVE construct. From leveraging the power of a tool like Twitter, to attending innovative educational events like the Tomorrow's Classrooms Today Conference. It's a life-long commitment to always finding a way to improve your craft as a coach who ultimately helps other educators be awesome! There is no doubt that this is not an easy process and that obstacles will have to be overcome again and again. But at the end of the day it's what's needed if the needs of a school's stakeholders are going to be met.

Following the EVOLVE framework will allow you to plan and make successful progress around your own professional growth. If people see you continuously evolving as a coach, then they, too, will rise to the occasion. When you commit to learning something new, ultimately others will get better at what they do. Evolve. Impact. Repeat.

Strategies and Resources for Continued Learning and Leading

Now that we have a framework for EVOLVEing as an educator, the next task is to figure out how to structure your learning. Let's consider a number of strategies and resources that you might employ on your learning journey.

Now, more than ever, coaches have an opportunity to evolve due in large part to technological advances. Social media has flattened the educational world and has provided coaches with an opportunity to share, reflect, collaborate, and push their game to the next level. Mobile devices connected to the internet have enabled coaches with an opportunity to access content or share ideas with a few taps of the screen or clicks of the mouse. It's no longer an option that coaches evolve in some way, shape, or form. Bottom line: status quo is not option. Educators from all walks of life, particularly instructional coaches, have something great to share that will impact or support another educator from a different part of the world.

Tech coaches cannot truly do their best work if they are not able to stay ahead of the technology curve. This means that coaches need to regularly take time to learn as part of their role. Luckily, the digital world provides tech coaches and leaders with a wealth of learning opportunities by becoming a "connected educator." As mentioned earlier in the chapter, leveraging the power of social media to gain exposure to best practice ideas and resources is necessary if solid support structures are to be in place to help colleagues move from good to great.

Figure 6.3 below shows one way coaches can systematically plan for their own learning using the EVOLVE framework.

In as little as 100 minutes a month (or a week if you are feeling ambitious), tech coaches can stay ahead of the curve and share with others what they are learning. Of course, the resources listed in this chart are not the only ones a tech coach or leader might harness for continuous improvement. There are so many resources available for tech coaches to explore.

Six platforms in particular can be of great help when looking for a place to start learning: Twitter, Instagram, Pinterest, LinkedIn, Voxer, and Facebook (Figure 6.4). They allow you to instantly and virtually join a coaching Professional or Personal Learning Network (PLN).

Figure 6.3 Sample Tech Learning Plan

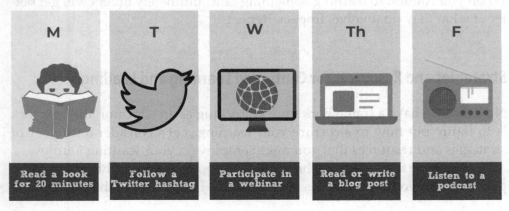

Figure 6.4 Virtual Coaching PLN Platforms

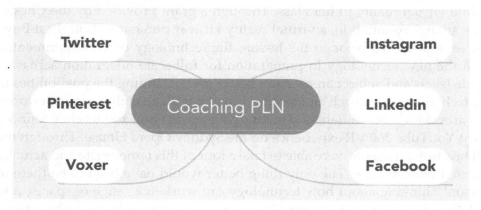

Twitter is a tremendous microblogging platform where people can share ideas, links, pictures, and videos in 280 characters or less. Instagram appeals to people who are more visual and learn by seeing actual postings. Pinterest provides users with a mechanism to create topic-specific boards where you can "pin" various online resources of interest to you. Voxer is a tap-to-talk app that gives users the ability to converse in real time or playback messages. LinkedIn is a professional-based social networking site that allows users to connect with other like-minded individuals. Facebook is probably one of the most popular social media platforms where people can connect with family, friends, and colleagues and share ideas, resources, and information of all kinds.

All of these platforms provide educators with a chance to connect with people they may or may not know. While it can seem odd at first to converse with people you do not know, it's amazing what you can learn and from whom you can learn it! Social media and technology have flattened the educational world—they have removed the barriers for collaboration with a wide range of individuals from all over the world—and you reap the benefit of that. Say, for example, you were assisting a colleague in finding ways to integrate virtual or augmented reality into an upcoming lesson. To learn more, you could go onto a platform like Twitter and search through hashtags like #VR, #AR, #VirtualReality, or #AugmentedReality. You would soon come across tweets posted by educators and non-educators. Even better, you can follow the people whose work interests you and tweet at them to learn more about what they are doing with VR or AR in educational spaces. Then, you take that information back with you to school and help your colleague plan an engaging learning experience.

You can also learn a great deal by collaborating with colleagues from all levels and disciplines in your school or district. For example, Brad observed a technology coach collaborating with a performing arts teacher to incorporate virtual reality in her class. Through a grant provided by the Chester Educational Foundation, a virtual reality kit was purchased from Best Buy.[2] For several weeks prior to the lesson, the technology coach experimented with the new technology in preparation for full-scale integration across all grade levels and subject areas. After better understanding the possibilities of the technology, the coach and teacher tested it with an eighth grade performing arts class. The students were studying operas and the teacher found a great YouTube 360 VR experience on the Sydney Opera House. Through the VR headsets, students were able to take a tour of this famous site and actually watch a performance. The only thing better would have been to be there in person! Thinking about how technology can work in a range of spaces, and collaborating with peers to experiment with that technology can be a fabulous learning experience as well.

Be a Lead Learner

A large part of coaching is modeling what it means to keep growing and learning and to support others in doing so as well. Therefore, we encourage you to include helping others learn as part of your action plans to achieve your goals. After all, keeping all that knowledge to yourself doesn't help! Consider how you can create venues for helping others learn about and try out best practices. Encouraging others to try is the only way to improve on a consistent basis and have a legitimate impact on student success. Here are four ways that instructional coaches support others professionally in and outside of the classroom setting:

1. *Hold a Smackdown.* Don't know what one is? A Smackdown is a sharing of websites, tools, or teaching tricks that you have found to be great to use. Each participant is given two minutes to present the tool to the group.[3] Smackdowns can easily be held at every faculty meeting, subject area meeting, grade-level meeting, and curriculum day throughout the school year. Sharing becomes contagious especially when you give a flashy name like Smackdown. Just because you work with someone in the same building does not mean you actually know all the great things going on in their classroom. Conducting a Smackdown at a faculty meeting will shed light on how your colleagues are using technology to engage and innovate.
2. *Blast out Weekly Email Digests.* Tech coaches can create or subscribe to weekly email digests that can be disseminated to staff in a timely fashion. For example, Brad blasts out a bi-monthly Bulldog

Bulletin to staff that contains best practice resources. He does this by scouring the web for articles and blogs. Then he adds the resources to a webpage that is housed on the district website.

3. *School Hashtag.* Create a school-wide or district-wide Twitter hashtag. This can be a tremendous help for staff as they look to improve their craft and find information easily via social media. #WeAreChester is a great way for staff to tell their classroom and school stories, but also serves as a form of professional development due to the types of experiences that are being posted on Twitter.

4. *Edcamps.* Edcamps provide an alternative way of sharing and learning. People show up at a location, have the freedom to hold a conversation on an educational topic, attend sessions that are applicable to their field of study, or get up and leave if they aren't interested in what's being presented.[4] You can attend a local Edcamp for free and be exposed to some of the most innovative ideas in education. Giving people the autonomy to learn what they want where they want is incredibly powerful. No longer is it an option for staff to stay on top of best practices by sitting them in a room and force-feeding them information. Chances are they will take the same approach with students in the classroom. Want to take it a step further as an instructional coach? Run your very own school or district-wide Edcamp.

The number of ways educators can grow, and help others grow, in this day and age is truly incredible. What you just read above is only a sample of the great resources that can make us all better in meeting the needs of diverse learners. Opening a magazine and reading about a best practice teaching technique just doesn't cut it anymore. Educators must be able to share, collaborate, discuss, and reflect on how they will push the envelope in order to promote the success of students. So take a few moments and really think how you could incorporate one of these ideas into your own professional life or within the school setting. There is no doubt that it will have a positive impact on your growth as an educator.

Reflecting on Progress towards Goals

John Dewey (1938) once said, "We do not learn from experience, we learn from reflecting on experience." He went on to explain that in the moment when things are happening to us, we simply react. We do not take time in that moment to understand the reaction or its consequences. Reflection, according to Dewey, therefore, is more critical than the experience itself. If we do not take the time after the experience to stop and reflect, we have missed the learning opportunity. Emily likes to say that one of the most important jobs of a coach is simply to hold space for coaching clients to reflect because it is the first thing to go out the window when we are busy (and educators are always busy). It is not just teachers that need space for reflection, however. It is also the coaches. For this reason, reflection is included as a critical component in the goal-setting process.

We encourage coaches to take time regularly to reflect and not wait only until a large goal is accomplished or after a significant length of time has passed. There are easy ways to quickly reflect on a daily (or more often) basis. One of Emily's favorite strategies is to create a personal log in which we record the answers to just four questions that are derived from the world of cognitive coaching:

1. What is working? Why?
2. What is challenging or drawing your attention now? Why?
3. What are you going to do next?
4. What supports do you need?

These deceptively simple questions have a lot of power and you will be amazed how asking others or yourself these questions can help make sense of situations and get the one answering them unstuck.

In addition to asking these questions of ourselves or others in a formative way, it's also critical to ask ourselves these questions at more summative points. You will notice that in the goal-setting template we shared at the beginning of this chapter, we included a space for reflection. The prompt reads, after completing the goal:

◆ Reflect on what specific actions/steps you made that helped you achieve your goal. Could any of these be replicated next time?
◆ Also consider what was challenging as you worked towards your goal. What might you improve next time?

You will note that these are derivatives of the same formative questions listed above. They provide coaches and leaders an opportunity to pause and consider what can be learned from this experience that will help improve the quality of the next experience.

We urge you to not let reflection fall off your "To Do" list when things get busy. It is the only thing, in reality, that leads to consistent improvement. If you truly want to stay ahead of the curve, reflection will help you focus clearly on where to spend your precious time and make you more efficient and effective as an educator, lead learner, and coach.

Putting It All Together

In this chapter, we've focused on the crucial role of continued learning in a rapidly changing technological world. We shared strategies for setting professional goals utilizing tech coaching standards and making action plans to achieve them. We've explored professional standards, the EVOLVE framework, and resources to help you grow towards your goals, and we've explored the power of reflection to help your continued professional learning journey. We hope you are walking away from this chapter with a plan that will truly help you stay ahead of the curve and be a strong contributor to your future-ready environments.

In the last chapter, we will consider the ever-widening range of ways tech coaches are seeing their roles grow that require them to not only be knowledgeable about best practices in teaching, learning, and technology, but also be able to think beyond any individual tool and consider the greater range of possibilities in ways that impact the broader educational system.

Notes

1 https://futureready.org/program-overview/coaches/ and www.iste.org/standards/for-coaches.
2 https://bit.ly/2nUnd8I).
3 You can read more about smackdowns at http://cybraryman.com/smackdown.html.
4 You can learn more about Edcamps here: www.edcamp.org/.

References

Currie, B., Krakower, W., & Rocco, S. (2016). *140 Twitter Tips for Educators: Get Connected, Grow Your Professional Learning Network, and Reinvigorate Your Career*. San Diego, CA: Dave Burgess Consulting.

Dewey, J. (1938). *Experience and Education. The Kappa Delta Pi Lecture Series*. New York: Touchstone.

7

New World Coaching
Leading System-Wide Innovation

Our director of teaching and learning went to a conference and learned about a new trend in school design which included using modular furniture and movable technology to create flexible classroom spaces. He asked the tech coaches in our district to help bring this idea to our district. None of us had ever done anything like that before. I mean, we aren't administrators, but we were excited about the idea, so we said yes. He sent us to visit other districts so we could see what it looks like, ask questions, and learn from their experts. We also went to a conference on rethinking school design which was really interesting. We asked the director to buy flexible furniture for two schools and see what happened. When we visited those classrooms, we were surprised to see that the teachers weren't doing anything different with the desks. They were still in rows or groups. I talked with one teacher about how you could make some of the desks standing desks and why you would do that. I also talked with her about using a second screen in the classroom so everyone could see the screen easily. She was interested but had not thought about those things! I realized we had forgotten a really important piece in trying something new—teaching the teachers how to use it. That's tough for me to say, as a coach, but it's true. At the end of the semester, when the district team went through and saw that the desks weren't being used differently, we lost our funding to bring flexible furniture to other classrooms. Even the director whose idea it was didn't back us. I realized there were a number of missteps we made with that project. That was a rough experience, but I learned a lot from it.

- Grace,[1] District Instructional Coach

In the past few years, tech coaches in many settings have seen their roles grow from supporting the use of individual technologies, infrastructure upgrades, or one-to-one device rollouts, to being tasked with larger initiatives like developing Makerspaces for schools, leading robotics and coding initiatives, integrating 3D printers, or implementing flexible classroom design efforts. Making the shift from coaching teachers or teams to leading school or district initiatives requires technology coaches to not only be knowledgeable about best practices in teaching, learning, and technology but also understand and navigate school or university systems as well as understand where these concepts fit in the larger field of edtech knowledge.

In this chapter we will:

◆ share a decision-making schema tech coaches can use when asked to lead system-wide projects;
◆ explore two real-world examples of this decision-making schema in action; and
◆ consider other digital education spaces in which the leadership of tech coaches is needed.

Our hope is you will leave this chapter with a better understanding of how to make the most of these new world coaching opportunities when they arise for you.

An Organizational Decision-Making Schema for Coaches

Coaches live in a unique world—they are not teachers, generally, nor are they administrators. They live between these two worlds and have the opportunity, as Emily's former director, Laura Gschwend, used to say, to "lead from the middle." Leading from the middle is an interesting position because it requires coaches to be able to understand and navigate two worlds—the world of classroom teaching and the world of school and district leadership—with equal ease. They must be able to speak both languages, understand both perspectives, and successfully interact with players in each of these domains. There is an expectation that you can switch from working down in the details with a teacher on a project to thinking about tech implementation in your district from a 10,000-foot view, and then back again with ease. Leading from the middle also means that people in both worlds will look to you as a go-between; as someone who can provide insight into the other world. As a result, coaches often get asked to be thought partners for leaders at all levels of the organization and, sometimes, they get asked to take on leadership for projects that they never would have dreamed of leading before. While most coaches still consider themselves teachers and think like teachers, coaches need to begin to look

Figure 7.1 Organizational Decision-Making Schema for Coaches

Vision Setting	Research and Development	Piloting	Scaling Up

1. What is the expected outcome?	1. Where/from whom can we learn?	1. Who should pilot? Selection?	1. Learnings from pilot?
			  a. What questions remain?
			  b. How will these be addressed?

2. Connected school/district goals?	2. Stakeholder input?	2. What must piloters do/share/gather?	2. What parameters are there for scaling up? Time? Resources? Size? Interest?
3. How will students be impacted?	3. How fit into schedule/curriculum?	3. Length of pilot?	3. How will we organize scale up?

4. How will teachers be impacted?	4. Where will it be located/organized?
	  a. How will it be set up?
	  b. What resources are needed?
		4. Funding of pilot?	4. Who will oversee scale up?

5. Who will be involved?	5. What technologies will work best?	5. What data will be collected?	5. What supports needed for implementation?

6. Stakeholder input on vision and goals?	6. Who will implement this?
	  a. Training/support need?
	  b. Who can train? Time? Cost?
	  c. Expectations for those trained?
		a. Who will collect data? When?
		  b. What will be done with data? When?
		  c. With whom will data be shared? When?
			6. What data will be collected, analyzed, shared? When? By with whom?

7. What is my role in this project?
  a. What are the expectations?
  b. Decision-making authority level?
  c. How much time will it take?
  d. Whom will I report to?
  e. Who can help me navigate the system?
	7. Who would use this?
	  a. Selection, training, support?
	  b. Who can train? Time? Cost?
	  c. Expectations for those trained?
	8. How long would it take to roll out?
		6. How will changes be made, if at all, during the pilot?
		7. How, when, and who will determine if next steps?
			7. How will we judge continued success?
			8. Scale up and ongoing funding?

beyond that role to understand the way the school works, how the district or university operates, as well as developing an understanding of what is going on in the broader world of education and how your work fits into those ideas.

We find that, because of the expertise that tech coaches possess, and the keen interest that schools have in making their systems more techie, tech coaches are getting tapped more frequently than other coaches with larger and larger leadership roles. In the opening vignette of this chapter, you read about a tech coaching team that was tasked by an excited district leader to implement a flexible classroom initiative. We can assume that the district leader valued the knowledge of Grace and her colleagues and invested in their learning. However, Grace and her team had never tried to lead a district initiative before and, as a result, they made some mistakes that led to the scrapping of this project by the district. Brad and Emily both can recount their own stories like this one and the trial and error ways in which they had to learn their jobs. I am sure everyone reading this who has made the move to another level of organizational leadership without support can empathize with what happened in this situation. It doesn't have to be like that, however.

Please know that we don't want these cautionary tales to scare you away from taking on these exciting and innovative projects. Instead, if you are offered the opportunity to spearhead a new initiative, we want you to take time to plan it out carefully. In Figure 7.1, we've shared a decision-making schema we developed that you can use to help you turn that exciting idea into a successful reality.

As you read across this continuum, you may have noticed two things:

1. the series of steps in the process; and
2. the set of guiding questions for each stage.

We cannot answer each of these questions for you as each initiative is different and the context of each organization is different. However, these stages and questions are universal to almost all new initiatives. Knowing the answers to these questions will increase the likelihood of your project's success.

Coaches as Researchers

A valuable skill coaches need to develop, whether working one-on-one with teachers, coaching teams, or leading initiatives is how to research, understand the possibilities of the technology or application, synthesize, and be able to instruct others on how to effectively integrate. Where can a coach start? As we have discussed throughout this book, having a strong network of educators on a platform like Twitter is one way to stay in tune with what technology has an impact on teaching and learning. On the same note, educators can research best practices by subscribing to such things as the *Marshall Memo* and *EdTech Magazine*. Another great resource for gaining insight into impactful technology is www.commonsensemedia.org. The bottom line is the instructional coaches must be on the forefront of what's happening in the educational world and be able to model the application of what they have learned to their colleagues.

Beyond the latest technologies, coaches also need to understand the deeper research around best practices in teaching and learning and how technology can support the implementation of such practices in classrooms. For example, John Hattie's book, *Visible Learning*, utilizes metadata research to synthesize thousands of studies to understand scientifically what actually makes a difference in student outcomes. As coaches, understanding this

Figure 7.2 Visible Learning in the Digital World Matrix

Domain	Influence	Effect Size	Technology	Application	Supporting Resources
Follow the #EdTechVL hashtag on Twitter					
Created by @TheBradCurrie					
Student	Deafness	−0.61	Google Slides Caption	Engage all audience members with captions	Present Captions with Google Slides
Teaching	Collective Teacher Efficacy	1.57	Twitter	Expand personal or professional network	140 Twitter Tips for Educators by Brad Currie, Scott Rocco, and Billy Krakower
Teaching	Feedback	0.7	Google Docs	Timely feedback during writing process	Docs Editors Help
Teaching	Classroom Discussion	0.82	Flipgrid	Video for student engagement and formative assessment	Common Sense Media Flipgrid Review
Teaching	Providing Formative Evaluation	0.48	Playposit	Interactive video to improve retention	Edtech Tip of the Week: Playposit
Teaching	Questioning	0.48	Mentimeter	Interactive presentations to engage audiences	Building Interactive Learning Environments
Teaching	Questioning	0.48	Socrative	Effective engagement and on the fly assessments	13 Ways to Use Socrative
Teaching	Concept Mapping	0.64	Mindmeister	Visualize your thoughts	How Concept Maps Help Deepen Learning
Learning Strategies	Summarization	0.79	Sutori	Presentations in the classroom using a unique timeline format	20 Ways to Use Sutori

research can have a profound impact on how teachers teach and students learn with technology. Take a look at the matrix Brad created that marries Hattie's work with educational technology (Figure 7.2).

How might a coach use this table? Let's take Hattie's research that shows classroom discussions have 0.82 effect size on student learning (that's a large effect size). A tech coach who is aware of this research can share this information with teachers and help them select technologies like Flipgrid, a private video response platform, to share their insight about a topic and listen and comment to their classmates' responses. At a larger district initiative level, knowing this research can help a coach provide research-based insight to a district team on where to invest limited resources in ways that will have the most impact on teaching and learning.

Now that we have a clearer understanding of how to make this schema more concrete, let's ground it in a set of examples.

Example 1: Makerspace Project

Over the past few years, Makerspaces have increased in popularity in schools. In the fall of 2014, Brad attended an Edcamp Leadership in North Jersey and participated in a Makerspace Think Tank conversation with other like-minded educators. The librarian at one of our middle schools, Janet Aaronson, also was introduced to the idea at a librarian's conference around the same time and was interested in integrating a Makerspace into her library. We decided we would plan to try out this idea in her library in the 2015–16 school year.

1. *Vision Setting*

    Our vision for the Makerspace was to help promote a "learning is messy" mentality for students and teachers which, we think, will help with our ultimate goal of promoting the success of all students. Further, the Makerspace experience, coupled with our STEM and Computer Application classes could support students as they make sense of the world they live in now and the unknowns of the future. We put together a team comprised of the school leader, district leadership, the librarian, and technology coaches to enact this project. The tech coaches were tasked from the beginning with supporting, directly or indirectly, the implementation of various technologies and web applications that students interact within the Makerspace.

2. *Research and Development*

    Throughout the rest of the school year, the team met on several occasions. We read research on Makerspaces including Laura Fleming's book *Worlds of Making* and her website http://

worlds-of-learning.com/. We reviewed Meredith Martin's website http://techforteachers.com/ and its plethora of resources related to the Maker Movement which helped to generate ideas within the confines of our own educational environment. Staff members were sent out to Makerspace workshops and visited schools that were dabbling in this new area of education. With all of this information, we then brainstormed ideas related to location, supplies, supervision, student schedules, and technology to name a few. We agreed that we needed to start small and, since the librarian was already interested, we agreed that she would manage the project. We also needed to find funding to help cover the supplies, materials, and technologies a Makerspace would require. Our board of education approved monies to help support the Maker Movement in our school. The Chester Education Foundation also awarded our school a few grants so we were able to purchase two 3D printers. Parents and community members donated supplies that the students could use to create and tinker.

3. *Piloting*

At the beginning of the 2015–16 school year, we launched the Makerspace in the middle school library and made it available to students during specific lunch periods and recess periods. Based on our research, we had the following items available for students to use:

- ◆ EduStation Pilot Pro Flight Simulator;
- ◆ Sphero App-Enabled Ball;
- ◆ Makey Makey Kits;
- ◆ Legos for Education;
- ◆ Dollar Store Supplies;
- ◆ FlashForge 3D Printer;
- ◆ Erector Super Construction Set;
- ◆ Cubelets;
- ◆ 3D Printing Pens;
- ◆ Arduino Kits; and
- ◆ Sewing Machines.

We gathered data on how many students were using the space, when they were using it, and what they were using it for. The librarian also kept track of how much time she was spending supervising the Makerspace and the impact of that on her workload. We also encouraged teachers to come and visit the Makerspace and consider how they might use it in their contexts. The Makerspace was quite popular and, as a result, we decided to try expanding the amount of time it was available to students before, during, and after the school day.

4. *Scaling Up*

At the end of the 2015–16 school year, the team met to review the data. It was clear that the Makerspace had been a positive addition to this library for a number of reasons including that the librarian was committed to its success. The participation numbers continued to rise throughout the school year. We brainstormed options for possible scale-up which included making the Makerspace an extension of our STEM class. Another possibility would be for classes to utilize the Makerspace to supplement their understanding of a particular topic. We decided to continue to run the Makerspace in the middle school library overseen by the librarian and supported by the tech coaches.

Makerspace-type experiences were also added to the elementary schools throughout the curriculum and as an extracurricular activity. Funding for the Makerspaces continues to come from the school budget and grants provided by the PTO and Ed Foundation.

This team, led by the librarian with support from the technology coaches and Brad, took time—almost two years—to carefully set the vision, gather input, research and learn, plan, and pilot this initiative before making the decision to scale. It's easy to want to rush through these steps to get to the implementation part. However, doing so can lead to missing important steps, or worse, having rollout failure and having to shut down a really promising project.

Let's look at a second, more complex, example of an initiative that coaches might be tapped to lead or support—digital curriculum development. Whereas Makerspaces are smaller and more contained projects, the development of a digital curriculum involves numerous decisions, stakeholders, and moving pieces to be considered.

Example 2: Build a Digital Curriculum

With many teachers and students using digital devices for learning, it's imperative they have access to engaging and relevant digital resources. Instructional coaches are often tasked with this type of initiative in districts because of their knowledge and skill. Let's take a look at how the development of curriculum might be rolled out and the areas a coach or leader would need to consider in such an endeavor.

1. *Vision Setting*

The purpose of creating and maintaining a digital curriculum is to foster innovation, creation, and critical thinking skills for students. This vision generally connects with school and district foci on ensuring teaching and learning thrive in the digital world by combining pedagogically sound methods with technology. The impact on students and teaching will be one that provides additional opportunities to reach every student so that they can show what they know about the topic at hand in a plethora of ways. When setting a vision around the development of a digital curriculum, it is important to involve school and district leadership, teaching staff, and, of course, technology coaches. Tech coaches will play an important role in supporting staff district-wide before, during, and after the digital curriculum transition as well as sharing back learning, ideas, and understandings from their lead role in implementing the initiative.

Coaches and leaders need to be clear about how this project will connect with larger district initiatives and how it will meet teacher and student needs. When establishing a vision for a digital curriculum you need to ask yourself the following questions:

◆ How will it engage students in meaningful and relevant ways?
◆ How will it push teachers to create innovative learning environments?
◆ How will it help address gaps and strengths as it relates to student performance?
◆ How will teachers be supported in this new way of life?
◆ What impact will it have on learning at home?
◆ What role do school and district leaders play in its success?

The vision for your school or district's digital curriculum must include keywords and phrases such as autonomy, choice, risk-taking, innovation, real-world application, collaboration, reflection, creation, curation, and paperless to name a few. The vision must focus on putting a new twist on old methods. From turning in assignments to real-time assessments to easily accessible content. No subject area should be left behind when looking at all the innovative ways your digital curriculum will transform learning spaces.

From vision setting, the team should move on to setting goals with input from all stakeholders including parents and community members. Digital curriculum goals should be student centered and focus on such things as differentiation, autonomy, creation, and collaboration. You will want to consider:

◆ Assessment: teachers must be able to gauge student comprehension of the topic in real time. There are many "tools of the trade" that provide users with this capability.

◆ Learning.:the main focus of your digital curriculum should be on how students can gain exposure to content at their own individual level.

◆ Usability: teachers must be able to thrive within the framework of your digital curriculum. They must be supported in a way that allows them to take risks and grow professionally on a consistent basis.

2. *Research and Development*

Once there is a vision in place, the team needs to develop a deeper understanding of what a successful digital curriculum will require. Strong research begins with an understanding of theory and best practices in the field. The team will need to consider what they can read and where they can go to learn more. With this theoretical and practically grounded understanding, the team will need to embark on answering questions about how this initiative will take shape in your context. There are no "right" answers to these questions. The way your team or school answers these questions will be totally dependent on your vision, your context, your budget, and your staffing. It is imperative that you answer them, however, before piloting. Let's take a look at the key factors that must be addressed in order to develop a sound digital curriculum:

a. Device Integration Plan: a key component of any successful digital curriculum initiative is device access. We understand that there are many factors that can impact the ability of a school or district to offer every student a device including funding and technological infrastructure. Even if you are able to secure these items, there still needs to be a plan in place to ensure that all stakeholders are able to utilize the devices in ways that meet their needs.

Let's start with the teacher's ability to successfully provide relevant learning experiences for students. Some key questions to consider as teachers plan for having students thrive with devices at their disposal:

◆ What procedures will students follow on a daily basis to ensure that their devices are taken care of and utilized where appropriate?

◆ How are the varying needs of students going to be met when devices and digital curriculum are meshed together?

◆ How will the teacher be supported from a professional growth standpoint?

◆ How will teachers gauge the effectiveness of the device integration and digital curriculum?

◆ What role will school and district leadership play in the success of the device integration plan?

The answers to the questions raised here are instrumental to the overall success of your plan. As an example, let's take a look at the impact that Chromebooks can have on a school's digital curriculum. A Chromebook is completely cloud-based and needs WiFi to work effectively. It runs off the Chrome browser and is linked to a user's Google account. Many schools lean towards Chromebooks due to their low cost and multiuser capability. It's important to remember that your school or district register for a G Suite for Education account. This way each staff member and student can have access to Gmail, Drive, and the hundreds of apps and extensions available in the Chrome store. The evolution of Google Classroom allows students to thrive in a paperless learning environment.

Another viable option is to purchase iPads for students and staff. iPads cost more but have more features than Chromebooks including touchscreen use. This capability is especially helpful for younger students who can more easily access curriculum by way of web applications with a few taps of the screen. IPads work better for learning experiences that incorporate stations or require mobility as well. However, as of the writing of this book, Apple has still not figured out a way to make the iPad multiuser friendly which makes it less useful for other applications.

A third option is BYOD or Bring Your Own Device. This lowers costs for districts as they do not have to purchase devices. Students bring their own device to school each day and tap into the filtered WiFi. However, students will bring a range of devices to school meaning that teachers and coaches will need to ensure applications are workable across a wide range of platforms. There are additional equity issues with BYOD to consider as well. If you work in a school with low-income students, they may not have access to a device which can further the access divide in your school instead of working to close it.

b. Resources to be included in the development phase: the implementation of a 21st-century digital curriculum needs to include a significant number of resources that school stakeholders can easily access. All subject areas must be considered and options provided that are suitable for a range of learners including students with special needs and English learners. Digital resources must be easily accessible in a virtual central location and provide staff with the ability to upload and/ or download with a few taps of the screen or clicks of the mouse. Sharing of best practices must be the centerpiece of any successful digital curriculum rollout. Historically, educators have worked in isolation, but with the evolution of technology, collaboration and sharing have become much easier. Resources should have the ability to be utilized across multiple subject areas, provide feedback to students in a timely fashion, engage learners in meaningful learning experiences, and be accessible on most devices that are connected to the internet. Teachers will also need ongoing coaching support to learn how to use these technologies as well as understand their collaborative possibilities.

Any successful digital curriculum will have the ability to differentiate resources for students and teachers. It's imperative that autonomy is at the forefront of digital learning experiences. For example, students in a language arts class must have the ability to show what they know about a certain book they are reading utilizing a plethora of web applications like Pear Deck, WeVideo, or Kahoot. These tools not only enhance comprehension for that particular student, but also the entire class. To that end, digital resources must be flexible and accessible to all stakeholders. The National Education Technology Plan released by the Department of Education explicitly supports digital learning experiences that address diverse learners. Speech-to-text features, read-aloud books, virtual reality devices, and so much more can promote the success of all students.

Social studies teachers can provide students with a blended learning experience utilizing a tool like Blendspace. Lessons can be built and pushed out digitally. Documents, websites, videos, content, and so much more can enhance students' learning experiences of the topic at hand. An important part of a robust digital curriculum is for teachers to have the ability to build lessons and share out to fellow colleagues or students.

Reading and writing are two important skills that all students need in order to be successful in life. Literacy across multiple disciplines must be a main focus of your digital curriculum. Teachers must differentiate the ways students tackle text by way of tablets, audiobooks, translation tools, and embedded assessments. From a writing perspective, students need access to tools that assist them in putting words on their devices. Speech-to-text capabilities build confidence within students, especially struggling writers. Utilizing the voice typing feature in Google Docs helps with writer's block and give students another option to express their thoughts.

Digital curriculum resources are the backbone to ensuring that learning environments are engaging, relevant, and meaningful. It's important to remember that there are thousands of apps, websites, and online programs. Which is why it's imperative that they are organized by subject area and grade-level on a central web page. It's also important to have your "go-to" websites that are updated daily with digital resources that can be used that day in class. Monica Burns' Class Tech Tips[2] website provides daily examples of how various iPad apps can be used to enhance student learning. Alice Keeler[3] does a phenomenal job of consistently pushing out content related to G Suite for Education and Google Classroom. Richard Byrne's Free Technology for Teachers[4] website provides tips on how to successfully integrate a wide array of edtech tools across all grade-levels and subject areas. Of course, these are just three of many relevant "go-to" sites to help support the teaching and learning goals of your school's digital curriculum.

c. Stakeholder Input Plan: any successful digital curriculum includes stakeholder input. Students, teachers, administrators, board of education members, community members, and parents must have a voice in making the digital curriculum engaging and relevant. There is no doubt that the digital curriculum will impact students and teachers the most, but it's imperative that an "all hands on deck" approach is taken to ensure that it's well rounded. Over the years technology has given stakeholders a way to be an integral part of a school's digital curriculum. Take for example how Mystery Location Calls can bring community members into your classroom so that students can learn about careers and geography.

Billy Krakower, Jerry Blumengarten, and Paula Naugle write about this innovation in *Connecting Your Students with The World*. Brad Currie once connected with an elementary class in New Jersey using FaceTime. Students asked probing questions to determine a location and gather insight on a career as an educator. Brad Currie's book, *All Hands on Deck: Tools for Connecting Educators, Parents, and Communities*, provides other alternatives to giving stakeholders a voice in the school setting.

So how can stakeholder input be gathered for your digital curriculum besides the typical meeting or planning session? Google Forms or Survey Monkey are great tools that can provide insight in an efficient manner. Specific feedback can be generated and guide the decision-making process with your digital curriculum. Conducting Google Hangouts or Skype sessions with your digital curriculum committee are viable alternatives as well, especially if meeting in person is not an option. These sessions can be recorded and viewed by committee members at a later time. In terms of building the actual curriculum, Google Docs allows multiple users to collaborate, write, and comment in real time. Slack is a team messaging service that can improve communication and efficiency for large groups that are working on a project like improving digital curriculum.

The most important stakeholder in the digital curriculum process is the student. Incorporating the students' voices is critical if meeting the needs of each and every student is the goal. For this to happen students need to be met where they are. There is no better place to engage students than on social media. Twitter, Instagram, and Snapchat are places where students reside in the virtual world. Seeking input on digital curriculum decisions through tweets, posts, and snaps can do wonders for making curricular decisions that are in the best interest of students. Questions, polls, and informational media can be blasted out to students through these social media channels.

3. *Piloting*

Putting your ideas into action on a small scale during the pilot phase allows you and your team to try ideas, resources, organizational strategies, and technologies in a controlled way and gather data on the impact of these decisions before scaling up. How can digital teaching methods be enhanced during the pilot phase of building out a digital curriculum? How can teachers best support student learning while adhering to the digital curriculum? In Chapter 3 we shared three frameworks that can provide coaches and teachers with guidance on how teachers can set their learning environments up to help promote the success of students in the digital world—TPACK, SAMR, and the Technology Use by Quadrant within the Rigor Relevance Framework. In Chapter 6 we discussed ISTE's coaching and teaching standards which are also useful for you to consult when making decisions about the intersection of instruction and technology.

There are two additional frameworks that might prove useful to you:

1. Eric Sheninger's "Pillars of Digital Leadership" focuses on how technology coupled with empowerment and autonomy can do wonders for an innovative school culture. It's important to remember that technology integration is only as successful as the teacher who values pedagogy and relationships.

2. The National Education Technology Plan released by the Department of Education provides a clear insight into what teaching, learning, and leading must look like in the 21st century. This innovative document provides sound advice on the important role technology plays in education. In conjunction with pedagogically sound teaching and a commitment to addressing every student's needs, technology can do wonders. Autonomous learning environments, accessibility tools, and access to relevant digital resources are all functions of an innovative learning environment. This educational document is full of digital curriculum resources and initiatives that can move your school or district from good to great.

4. *Scaling Up*

If your pilot goes successfully enough, it's time to consider scaling your concept. Moving from small scale to larger scale brings with it excitement as well as new challenges and opportunities. Let's take a look at a few that might arise when developing a digital curriculum:

a. How can a digital impact plan and assessment tool drive future decisions? Status quo is never an option. So how does a district move forward once their digital curriculum is in place? Constant analysis and feedback are needed in order to inform future curricular decisions. What better way to do this than by leveraging the power of digital tools to gather insight on what works well and what needs improvement. An emphasis on skills students acquire within the digital curriculum framework is a must. So should student engagement with devices and the impact of professional development opportunities associated with highly effective tech integration. A combination of teacher and student input coupled with field observations can help create a clearer picture of what is helping students succeed in the digital world. Assessment data should also drive decisions particularly if they are tied in some way to the technology that is being utilized with the digital curriculum. Once data is collected, decisions can be made regarding the purchasing of devices, online programs, and professional development offerings. The correct decisions can only be made if the process is handled correctly.

b. How can personal learning networks (PLNs) and professional learning communities help enhance the digital curriculum in the future? Instructional coaches will often look for a place that has like-minded educators to talk shop and find solutions to address pressing issues. Every Saturday morning at 7:30 EST on Twitter, hundreds of educators share their insight on #Satchat. Topics that are discussed include educational technology, the whole-child approach to learning, digital resources, and school culture to name a few. Questions are shared out and answered using a Q1/A1 format. Over the course of the hour, thousands of tweets containing valuable advice and resources are made available to participants. Leveraging the power of social media, in this case, Twitter and the #Satchat hashtag, can help expand an educator's PLN and ultimately add value to what schools are trying to accomplish with their digital curriculum.

There are vast amounts of resources, by way of blogs, related to assessment, instructional coaching, Google Apps for Education, and passion-based learning to name a few. Starr Sackstein's blog does a tremendous job of providing educators with a unique perspective on assessment, particularly through the lens of educational technology.[5] Peter Dewitt's blog, *Finding Common Ground*, provides guidance on a host of educational topics including instructional coaching, intervention, ability grouping, data analysis, and standardized assessments. Eric Sheninger's blog, *A Principal's Reflections*, provides guidance for school leaders who are looking to thrive and support others in the digital world. These blogs and countless others are shared often throughout educator's PLNs and on social media sites like Twitter. There is no doubt that the educational world has come out of isolation over the last several years. Taking advantage of these types of networks will not only help you grow as educators but move your digital curriculum forward in a positive direction.

Professional learning communities (PLCs) can provide educators with an opportunity to move their digital curriculum forward once it's established. The utilization of technology can help facilitate collaboration, learning, and reflection within PLCs. Take for example G Suite for Education, in particular, Google Classroom. Once your PLC is established in the physical world, sharing and collaboration can take place in the virtual world throughout the school year. Digital curriculum resources can be posted and virtual conversations conducted with a few clicks of the mouse or taps of the screen.

There is no doubt that this is one of the most exciting times in education. Technology has the ability to level the playing field for so many parts of the educational process. A viable and living digital curriculum can be established in no time with the correct guidance and support from an instructional coach. Due to the fact that students are going to enter a world where they will be required to thrive with the help of technology, it's in the best interest of our collective school communities to come together and make certain that all the digital parts are in place to make these dreams become reality. Through a forward-thinking mind-set from an instructional coach and a commitment from teachers to providing innovative educational experiences, an all-encompassing digital curriculum can do wonders for student achievement.

Other Digital Education Spaces in which Tech Coach Leadership is Needed

Makerspaces and digital curriculum development are just two of the many examples of places in which the knowledge, coaching skill, and leadership of tech coaches can make a positive impact on teaching and learning. Below is a list of other common ways in which tech coaches can lead for change in their organizations:

1. *Supporting Struggling Learners*
    Tech coaches can help teachers reach struggling learners with various forms of technology. For example, I&RS (Intervention and Referral Services) take place to brainstorm best practices and put an action in place to meet the needs of struggling learners. A team of teachers, parents, administrators, guidance counselors, child study team members, and others convene to problem-solve student deficiencies. Below you will find a sampling of strategies

and technologies that tech coaches can recommend for students throughout the school year in order to put them in a position to be successful:

◆ Leverage the power of ClassDojo to track students' performance and behavior. This great tool can be very beneficial for students and parents in terms of communication, transparency, and buy-in.

◆ Encourage students to utilize their personal computer in the school setting for organization and curation purposes. Often students feel more comfortable using their own device as they make sense of their learning.

◆ Utilize the text-to-speech feature on Google Docs so that students can highlight their oral abilities on paper and/or computer screen.

◆ Increase mental agility at home while at the same time providing breaks with an Apple Watch or timer feature on the iPhone.

◆ Focus on increasing typing speed using a program called EduTyping. This program can be utilized at home and in school.

◆ Provide students with alternative assessment opportunities to show what they know on a given topic. For example, use the Book Creator app for a project in language arts.

Leveraging the power of technology and available web applications to promote the success of students is critical. Identifying student strengths in order to overcome weaknesses is important if schools are to put students in a position to be successful. There is no doubt that struggling students will do a complete turnaround and begin enjoying school once again.

2. *Measuring Student Learning*

Tech coaches must also understand and be ready to support the use of technology to measure student learning in an effective and timely manner. There are various resources and web tools that can help teachers truly impact student comprehension. Let's take a look:

a. The National Education Technology Plan, released by the Department of Education, which we discussed before, can also be a useful resource in this context. Within the plan, there are five key components that are addressed: learning, teaching, leadership, assessment, and infrastructure. All five of the components are incredibly important to learning and teaching, but some would argue that assessment plays the most crucial role in promoting the success of students. Measuring student learning is a very deep and complex topic. Over the years though, technology has provided educators with more viable options to administer assessments and obtain quality feedback within a more reasonable time frame. Below are four web tools that make measuring learning fun, informative, and engaging.

b. Plickers is a simple tool that allows teachers to gather data on student comprehension with little technology. Simply visit www.plickers.com and sign up for a free account. Then, set up your classes with as little or as much information that you see fit. The neat part about Plickers is that it requires a set of placards that contain QR code type images to be printed out from the website. These placards are then handed out to the class and used to answer questions that are pushed out from the website. So where does the assessment piece come into play? Download the Plickers app onto your smartphone or tablet and sync it with a virtual class you set up on the website. Then project the questions you created on the big screen in your classroom. As students read the questions they will hold up their placard a certain way based on the answer they want to give. The teacher will then scan the room with the Plickers app that was downloaded. In real time, both the teachers and students will see results from the questions posted on the topic at hand. Plickers is a great mix of old school and new school techniques to gather data and help address learning gaps in real time.

c. Playposit provides users with an opportunity to embed questions within video clips. Visit www.playposit.com and start embedding questions to videos that you find on sites such as YouTube. You can also utilize question-embedded videos that have been created by other educators. How powerful would it be for teachers to truly understand if their students really comprehend what they are watching in real time? Gone are the days of students just watching a video and answering follow-up questions on an as-needed basis. With eduCanon, students can watch a video and check for understanding at various points with a few taps of the touchpad. Struggling with a certain math concept? No problem. Access a related video through the search box and interact with the content by answering questions in real time.

d. Pear Deck is an interactive presentation tool that allows teachers and students to assess in real time. Visit www.peardeck.com and sign in with your Google account to get started. There are various question types that can be embedded within the slide deck you create including draggable, drawing, multiple choice, free text response, and free number response. Once the slide deck is created it can be pushed out to students' devices and accessed through a link that is given by the teacher. As the class makes their way through the interactive presentation the teacher can look on their dashboard for data in order to drive instruction in real time. Other websites like Kahoot, TED, and Popplet can be embedded in a slide deck.

e. Flipgrid enables teachers to create grids of questions or topics using text or video and then share with students. Visit www. flipgrid.com to register for a free trial and set up your very own virtual classroom. Once signed up, the teacher can start their very own discussion by recording a short video clip that contains a question which is then pushed out to the class. Students then respond to the question by recording and posting their video clip. All of the interactions are archived and viewed within the grid that the teacher created. Responses can also be shared out for others to view outside of the virtual classroom if warranted. Flipgrid is a great tool to build community, foster collaboration, and assess student comprehension in real time.

There are many options available for educators to leverage the power of technology in order to measure student learning. Plickers, Playposit, Pear Deck, and Flipgrid are just a few "tools of the trade" that can make assessment fun and meaningful. Over the next several weeks and months consider piloting one of these tools with your coaching clients and encourage them to hand over the keys to students and have them drive their own learning with these various web applications.

3. *Supporting Leadership in the Digital World*

School and district leadership in the 21st century requires a commitment to promoting the success of students in the digital world coupled with a heightened focus on pedagogy. This can only be done with the assistance of a talented tech coach who can guide a leader to see what is possible when technology is infused through all facets of an educational environment. More and more schools are going to BYOD or one-to-one to provide students with a more innovative learning experience. From firsthand experience, it has become quite obvious that students thrive in a world that promotes curation, collaboration, creativity, and communication. Of course, none of this can happen unless there is a culture that truly is passionate about doing what's best for kids. A caring attitude towards students, coupled with an innovative vision that is real-world appropriate can go a long way for all involved.

Putting It All Together

As districts, schools, and other organizations strive to adapt to a tech-centric world, tech coaches become an increasingly valuable commodity. They understand teaching and learning with technology, and they can also take on leadership to help drive new initiatives forward from their place of middle leadership. The new world of coaching responsibilities is not easy, however. Coaches need to understand how initiatives are developed, researched, piloted, and implemented in their systems so that they are able to successfully guide new ideas into reality for teachers and students. We hope this chapter has provided you with a framework and concrete examples of how coaches can thoughtfully shepherd ideas from theory to reality in their systems.

Notes

1 Pseudonym.
2 Monica Burns Class Tech Tips https://classtechtips.com/.
3 Teacher Tech with Alice Keeler https://alicekeeler.com/.
4 Richard Byrne's Free Technology for Teachers: https://www.freetech4teachers.com/.
5 Work in Progress on Education Week Teacher. Here is the link: https://blogs.edweek.org/teachers/work_in_progress/.

References

Association of Middle Level Education. (2012). *This We Believe in Action: Implementing Successful Middle Level Schools, 2nd Edition*. Westerville, OH: Association of Middle Level Education.

Currie, B. (2015). *All Hands on Deck: Tools for Connecting Educators, Parents, and Communities*. Thousand Oaks, CA: Corwin.

Fleming, L. (2015). *Worlds of Making: Best Practices for Establishing a Makerspace for Your School*. Thousand Oaks, CA: Corwin.

Hattie, J. (2009). *Visible Learning: A Synthesis of Over 800 Meta-Analyses Relating to Achievement*. New York: Routledge.

Krakower, B., Blumengarten, J., & Naugle, P. (2016). *Connecting Your Students with The World: Tools and Projects to Make Global Collaboration Come Alive, K-8*. New York: Routledge.

Office of Educational Technology. (January 2017). Reimagining the Role of Technology in Education: 2017 National Education Technology Plan Update. Washington, DC: US Department of Education.

Sheninger, E. (November 2014). Pillars of Digital Leadership. International Center for Leadership Education. Retrieved from: www.leadered.com/pdf/LeadingintheDigitalAge_11.14.pdf.

Conclusion

Schools, universities, and other educational organizations understand the transformational possibilities that integrating technology into education can engender, and are clear about the necessity of helping all students know how to access and effectively utilize technologies in preparation for the world of work. They have spent fortunes purchasing technologies and application subscriptions. They have taken out bonds to expand internet access and speed. Yet, the ways in which these technologies are being utilized, on the whole, is underwhelming. Chromebooks and iPads are used sporadically as replacements for paper and pencil, and Smartboards are left gathering dust in the corner of rooms. Enter tech coaches.

The research is clear. If organizations want to significantly increase the success of their initiatives, they must invest in long-term quality coaching for those tasked with enacting the initiative. When coaches are well trained and clear about their roles, they can not only drastically improve the speed at which technologies are integrated into classrooms, they can also help educators to meaningfully harness the power of technology to help them more efficiently and elegantly meet their teaching and learning goals in ways that are not possible without these tools.

These things don't happen by accident, however. Successful coaching programs are developed and sustained when:

1. *Tech coaches, and everyone else in the system, understand their role and value.* The way coaches are selected, their understanding of the parameters of their role, and their clarity about the outcomes for which they are accountable help to sharpen the coach or program's focus. When all stakeholders—district officials, school leaders, and teachers are also clear about the value of the program and how it can support improved teaching and learning, the work gets even stronger because everyone is brought into a common vision.

2. *Stakeholders understand good coaches are developed not born.* Just because a teacher is strong with technology in her own class does not ensure that she will be able to effectively coach other educators to do the same in their classrooms. Good coaches have a unique skill set of mind-sets, frameworks, protocols, language, and tools upon which they can draw to create meaningful and personal learning experiences for others. They know how to ask questions and truly

seek to understand the needs of others, they know how to structure conversations to grow the knowledge and skills of others, and they have a host of resources available at their disposal to provide support. These are things coaches need to be explicitly taught. These are skills that develop over time and through repeated support and practice. Effective coaching programs will ensure there is a comprehensive professional learning system in place to support coaches in developing these skills.

3. *Pedagogy comes first, and tech second.* Effective tech coaches are masterful instructional designers who understand the positive supports that technology can provide for teaching and learning. They are also clear that technology in education is not an end in and of itself. They know how to help educators use frameworks like TPACK and SAMR to think about the appropriate place of technology in teaching and learning, and know how to help teachers select tech resources that will be most useful in helping students reach their goals. They can articulate the possible interrelationships between social-emotional learning (SEL), 21st-century learning, educational equity, and technology. They also can help others see the ways in which technology can help parents become more fully vested partners in the teaching and learning process.

4. *Tech coaches can expand their support to teams of all sizes.* Facilitating professional learning for groups of educators, whether in a one-day session or regularly over time, requires new skills for coaches to learn, but also provides the system as a whole access to their expertise in new and exciting ways. Effective coaching programs will help create meaningful structures for teams and staffs to learn from tech coaches and will support tech coaches in learning the presentation and facilitation skills that will ensure their work has the greatest possible impact.

5. *There is a clear plan for gathering and sharing data for the purpose of continued program improvement and sustainability.* Understanding what can be collected and how it can be analyzed, shared, and utilized to strengthen the coaching program, outcomes for teachers and students, and further school and district initiatives is critical for success.

6. *Coaches know how to keep learning and growing.* To truly help others, coaches must first have a plan to help themselves. Setting goals, creating action plans that help coaches evolve, and harnessing the power of in-person and virtual learning networks to stay current in the rapidly changing world of technology, and taking time to reflect on progress and refine processes, is a crucial part of coaching.

7. *Coaches know how to look beyond their roles to the broader field and help lead their districts into the new world.* As organizations continue to realize the potential of technology to fundamentally transform education, they increasingly rely on tech coaches to serve as experts in the wide array of areas that tech touches. Tech coaches need to be able to serve as go-betweens in their systems. They must simultaneously be the voice of educators in the system while also understanding how their systems work and where they can lead for change. They need to be able to think beyond their own settings and experiences to understand possibilities and their ripples, and help others step into the new world tech can offer with them.

We hope that whether you are a district, school, or program leader, a university faculty member, or a new instructional coach, that this book has provided you with a schema for thinking about what effective tech coaching truly entails. Whether you are brand new to this role or have been working in the field for a while, we hope you are walking away with concrete ideas, resources, examples, and protocols that can guide your work and help you take it to the next level. We also want to thank you for taking on the task of coaching your peers to imagine their work in new ways. We know leading from the middle is not easy some days, but we also know how rewarding it can be. Keep learning, keep growing, keep leading. The future of our students depends on it.

Please stay connected with us: #TechRequestEDU.